The How-To Book of Evangelization

The How-To Book of
Evangelization

Everything
You Need to
Know but No
One Ever
Taught You

JENNIFER FITZ

Nihil Obstat
Msgr. Michael Heintz, Ph.D.
Censor Librorum

Imprimatur
✠ Kevin C. Rhoades
Bishop of Fort Wayne-South Bend
March 20, 2020

Except where noted, the Scripture citations used in this work are taken from the *Revised Standard Version of the Bible — Second Catholic Edition* (Ignatius Edition), copyright © 1965, 1966, 2006 National Council of the Churches of Christ in the United States of America. Used by permission. All rights reserved.

Every reasonable effort has been made to determine copyright holders of excerpted materials and to secure permissions as needed. If any copyrighted materials have been inadvertently used in this work without proper credit being given in one form or another, please notify Our Sunday Visitor in writing so that future printings of this work may be corrected accordingly.

Our Sunday Visitor Publishing Division
Our Sunday Visitor, Inc.
200 Noll Plaza
Huntington, IN 46750
1-800-348-2440

ISBN: 978-1-68192-355-0 (Inventory No. T2045)
1. RELIGION—Christian Theology—Apologetics.
2. RELIGION—Christian Life—General.
3. RELIGION—Christianity—Catholic.

eISBN: 978-1-68192-356-7
LCCN: 2019953158

Cover and interior design: Lindsey Riesen
Cover art: Shutterstock

PRINTED IN THE UNITED STATES OF AMERICA

To Jesus Christ

Table of Contents

Introduction

Many of us Catholics struggle to understand what evangelization and discipleship look like in real life. We've all heard the words, and we're pretty sure they stand for something important to us. We love being Catholic, and we want to share that love!

And yet many of us come from parishes that are closing down, due to supposedly inevitable decline. Others live in parishes that are holding steady, but sometimes steady feels more like stagnant. Still other parishes are seeing numerical growth, primarily due to an influx of newcomers from other regions of the country or the world. Many of us watch as generation after generation of our loved ones drift away from the Faith.

We can look around our parishes and see good people working hard to share God's love as best they know how. All this work, though, isn't quite working. We watch our society deteriorate, family life stretch and break, violence and addiction spread. Old evils such as racism and human trafficking still plague us even as new forms of suffering seem to pop up every year. We know that God doesn't want all this heartache for our world.

We know in our hearts it isn't supposed to be this way.

We know that we love Jesus, and he wants us to share that

love with the world.

We know there is a better way to live now and for all eternity.

We know that our faith offers true, lasting happiness.

So how do we succeed at sharing that faith with those around us?

Generation after generation, Catholics have to answer this question. The Church in her wisdom lays out a plan for evangelization as old and reliable as the words of Our Lord. Countless men and women across twenty centuries, from every walk of life and every corner of the globe, have lived out the mission God has given us: "And Jesus came and said to them, 'All authority in heaven and on earth has been given to me. Go therefore and make disciples of all nations, baptizing them in the name of the Father and of the Son and of the Holy Spirit, teaching them to observe all that I have commanded you; and behold, I am with you always, to the close of the age' " (Mt 28:18–20).

Our clergy lead this mission in a particular way, but all Catholics share in this work. You don't have to be a cleric or a religious to learn how to evangelize and make disciples. You don't need a theology degree. You don't need to be able to wade through the many priceless (but not always easy to read) treasures of the Doctors of the Church. God doesn't require you to be dazzlingly smart or famously holy. You might be a parish priest who barely squeaked through seminary, a religious education dropout, or a miserable wretch who's always haunting the confessional, aware of just what a lousy Catholic you are. Maybe you're the not-so-bad or even pretty-good Catholic, answering your vocation from day to day but sometimes wondering if God might want more of you.

God's plan for the Church was made to be carried out by ordinary Catholics like us, whatever our personal struggles. Evangelization and discipleship are the natural outflowing of who we are as persons who love Jesus Christ.

Think of someone you have loved, whether as a child, a sibling, a parent, a spouse, or a friend. The act of loving someone involves decisions and actions that flow from one's heart relationship with that person. If you've ever had to work on holding together a healthy friendship, marriage, or parent-child relationship, you know that learning some good relationship skills is helpful. The same is true in evangelization and discipleship: our innate love of God can be communicated and acted upon by learning ways of relating to others that help draw all of us closer to Jesus Christ.

These are skills that we the Church have been practicing for two thousand years and successful parishes around the world are using today, in cities and states and countries like yours. They are skills meant to be practiced by you and me, ordinary Catholics with a love for Jesus.

The skills and best practices we'll look at cover vast territory. Some skills will come naturally to you, and others will be more daunting. Some best practices will be perfect for your parish or community, and others simply don't have your name on them at this time. As you read the book, ask the Lord to shed light on those areas where he's asking you to step out in faith.

We'll begin with the key question: What exactly is evangelization? Then we'll examine briefly the two nonnegotiables of evangelization: prayer and fasting. The realities laid out in these three short opening chapters are the everything of evangelization; if you learn nothing else, learn these realities.

We'll continue our preparation in part 1 by examining our own lives, and then see how letting go of a program mentality frees us to evangelize more effectively by learning to view evangelization as a one-soul-at-a-time endeavor. Finally, we'll conclude our preparatory chapters with our first and most important soul-to-soul skill: listening effectively to the person you are trying to help.

In part 2, we'll move into the *how* of evangelization. We'll begin with fundamental skills and frameworks to help you listen to and understand the person you are trying to reach, whether a close friend or a family member, a neighbor, a colleague, someone you see around town or a stranger on the internet, or quite possibly someone you worship with every week at church. Each person you encounter has a story of his or her relationship with God, and the better you can understand that story, the better you can help that person discern the next steps in that relationship.

Then we'll explore different approaches and techniques of evangelization that belong in your toolkit. Some of our tools, such as apologetics, the works of mercy, or proclaiming the kingdom, will be relevant to all Catholics, even to those who are more gifted in one area than in another. Other issues we walk through, such as the how-tos of evangelization in the liturgy, at retreats, on the streets, or in the workplace, will speak to specific states in life. Give those specialized chapters a look even if they don't seem to apply to you right now; you will glean ideas you can use in your own situation and gain insight into the challenges that your sisters and brothers in the Faith reckon with day in and day out. We'll wrap up part 2 by looking at the moment when someone makes a conscious decision to follow Jesus Christ in the Catholic Faith and how to support that person when difficulties arise.

Finally, after all that work of evangelizing, in part 3 we'll delve into the whys and how-tos of discipleship. We often pair the terms "evangelization" and "discipleship," and indeed, they go hand in hand. So why do we wait until the final section of the book to look at discipleship? Think of the two terms in the context of taking a journey toward Jesus Christ. Evangelization is the path to Jesus Christ; it is everything that happens on the way to the encounter with the Lord that changes your life forever. Discipleship is what happens when you finally get there. You've fallen in love with your Savior and given your life to him, but now what?

"Discipleship" refers to three interrelated answers to that question. It refers to my life as someone living for Jesus; to the things that other Christians do to help me become a better Christian; and to the things that I do, in turn, to mentor and support my fellow disciples.

In answering that "Now what?" question, we'll be headed right back to the beginning. Disciples are people who love Christ, who adore Christ, and who serve Christ. Disciples are people whose prayer and action draw other souls toward Jesus. Disciples are people who evangelize.

You can be that disciple. You can evangelize. Let's get started.

Part 1

The Fundamentals

Part 1 is where we figure out how to become evangelists. We'll start with answering the big question, **What Is Evangelization? (chapter 1)**

Then we'll lay the foundation stones of our lives as evangelists: **Prayer (chapter 2), Fasting (chapter 3),** and **Integrity (chapter 4).**

Next, we'll have to let go of a little baggage in **Deprogramming (chapter 5).**

Finally, we'll wrap up by learning the single most important skill an evangelist brings to the mission field, **Listening (chapter 6).**

Once we've done all that, we'll be ready for **Part 2: How to Evangelize.**

1

What Is Evangelization?

So many good Catholic works get stamped with the same all-purpose label of "evangelization." What does that word really mean? In this chapter, we'll tackle the question of evangelization from a variety of angles. When we put it all together, we'll have a better idea of what it is that evangelists do.

Key Points

- Evangelization consists of the things we do to help others discover the lasting peace and joy of an intimate, personal relationship with Jesus Christ in the Catholic Faith.
- Evangelization requires concrete action.
- Evangelization is much more than "church growth" or merely filling pews.
- The people we know are not problems to be solved but persons to be loved.
- Evangelization is carried out one soul at a time.

Let me tell you the story of two conversions.

I was born and raised somewhat Catholic, and that up-bringing gave me a bridge of trust with the Catholic Church. As a young adult, I left the Faith, even as people around me were quietly evangelizing me. Most of that work was almost invisible: prayer, example, and encouragement when I was inching in a good direction.

Some evangelization was gentle but focused. I remember a priest, a friend of my great-great-aunt, chatting with me on a dock in Florida over spring break, encouraging me to read the Bible. Another Christian friend patiently let me ramble about religious topics, sometimes inserting a word of direction, but mostly just acting as my sounding board.

Some of the work was done directly by God. Ultimately, he showed me my loneliness without him, and he prompted me to begin actively seeking him again.

And finally, there was a very explicit moment of conversion. One morning, I sat down to a meeting with a client, and in the chit-chat I brought up something we had been discussing in our many conversations about Christianity. He felt the Holy Spirit prompting him to act. In the space of ten minutes, he led me to an explicit, overt decision to give myself to Jesus Christ. We prayed together, and then I was filled with an overwhelming desire to attend Mass as soon as possible.

That was my conversion. From there, the priest who said that first Mass I attended after my conversion ended up being the person who led me all the way back into the Catholic Faith.

Now for the other story.

My husband, Jon, was with me through all this. When we met, he wasn't practicing any religion. He saw me arrive at college and begin struggling with my faith. He talked me through the question of religion as we were considering getting married. Whereas I was spiritually restless, he was easygoing and accommodating; if I wanted a church wedding, he'd do it, or we could skip that. Up to me. He was there as I actively rejected Christianity, and when I expressed a desire for some kind of religion — I was open to a variety of options — he was the one who suggested that since we lived in a Christian culture, we should begin with some kind of Christian faith. As I sought God passionately and fitfully, he seemed to be drifting along in calm waters, letting the Holy Spirit gently ease him onto course.

He had many conversations with Christian friends, but no single moment he could point to and say was his conversion. And yet somehow he went from cradle-Catholic-turned-agnostic to church-going, Bible-loving evangelical Christian, but firmly in the Protestant camp. From his point of view, he had spent years surrounded by Catholics and never heard the Gospel, so the Gospel must not be found in Catholicism. After my reversion, I strongly disagreed, but I couldn't argue away his lived experience, no matter how much I wanted it to be something different.

Because of his feeling of having missed out on Jesus in his Catholic childhood, for years after my abrupt return to the Catholic Church, Jon was an ardent non-Catholic Christian. We argued about our religious differences — or, more accurately, I argued at him, and he endured it. I prayed for his conversion. Other Catholic friends prayed as well. And then I gave it up. I realized I needed to hand the situation over to God. I would continue to discern what part God wanted me to play in all this, but ultimately, changing Jon's heart was something that had to happen in *his* relationship with the Lord, not something I could fix if only I did all the right things at all the right times.

Despite my strident temper when it came to apologetics, Jon's faith slowly grew. He could see the biblical foundations of certain Catholic beliefs and practices. He would attend certain Catholic services. He and I had to work through numerous disagreements about how to rear our children in the Christian faith. Then, one morning, he came with the children and me to an ordinary Sunday Mass, rather than going to his Protestant congregation's service. Why? To get an extra half hour of sleep.

He came again the next week, and the next, and by the end of the month, I suggested perhaps he might like to go to confession.

Slowly, seamlessly, with no one single moment anyone could point to as his conversion, six months later Jon was calling himself Catholic. He never turned back. Bit by bit, over yet more years of soaking up Catholicism, he worked through the last of his discomfort with certain traditional Catholic practices, such as Marian devotion and the granting of indulgences. In every instance, Jon's conversion has always been one of easing into the Faith.

Two different personalities, two different paths of conversion. What do we have in common?

Both of us were evangelized.

Evangelization Means Concrete Action

Evangelization consists of the things we Christians do in order to help other people become Christians.

You can evangelize deftly, like my colleague who was so attuned to the promptings of the Holy Spirit, or you can evangelize clumsily, like me in my incessant arguing with my husband. One way or another, evangelization requires concrete, targeted action.

When we evangelize, we aren't just vaguely hoping that somehow something in our life will be of some possible help to others. Think of it like fixing a flat tire. Recently, I met up with friends for my daughter's carpool, and one of the other parents noticed my tire was low. He pointed out the problem with concern and offered to help me put on my spare. Well, yes, that tire has given me trouble before, probably a slow leak, I argued. Honestly, I'm not too diligent about maintenance; the tire was probably low and I had failed to notice, and anyway I was close to home. I happily let his son pump it up with the bicycle pump I keep in my trunk.

I got the car home, and my husband and I debated what to do. Attempt to patch it ourselves? We decided to take it to the tire shop, where it would probably need to be replaced. The mechanic assured me that he had attempted to repair it, and when it turned out that the tire could not be salvaged, he replaced it instead.

How does evangelization compare to the tire incident?

First and foremost, everyone in the long chain of people who helped solve the tire problem recognized a specific goal (a fully inflated, fully functioning tire) and took steps to achieve that goal. There was no wishing that our attitude of openness to fully inflated tires would somehow rub off on the universe, causing proper tire pressure to enter my life at the opportune moment.

Now, note that not everyone could do everything. One of our friends in the parking lot was probably praying for that tire, truth be told (I have good friends!). She might have prayed that I got home safely, prayed that we'd know what to do, prayed for an honest mechanic — but she would have prayed for specific requests related to the goal.

Likewise, the dad and son who initially helped couldn't do everything. It was up to me to be open to their help, first of all (I kept turning down that offer to get out the spare), and secondly, they couldn't see the problem through from start to finish, as they had other obligations. But to the extent that they could help, the question was always: Is this kind of help taking us in the right direction? Is it getting us closer to our goal?

As we ran into difficulties, we had to assess and change plans. We didn't just give up and decide that God wanted us to live with a flat tire and that was fine. Maybe it would cost more, or take more time, than we had hoped. Maybe we'd have to work out an alternative temporarily. Had we, for some reason, been unable to fix the tire, we wouldn't have decided to give up on transportation and stay home for the rest of our lives. When you are serious about addressing a significant problem in your life, you don't rest until you've achieved your goal.

In the same way, if we want to help people satisfy their innate spiritual drive, we'll want to take specific, concrete steps to help them find their way toward Jesus Christ in the Catholic Faith.

In the chapters ahead, we'll learn what those steps look like and how to discern what kinds of steps to take in which situations.

More Than a Numbers Game

So what exactly is the goal we're working toward? It's easy to know the goal when it comes to a flat tire. What is the goal when it comes to Jesus Christ?

"Evangelization" is often used to mean "filling the pews" or "church growth." We imagine we want to take concrete action to achieve measurable results: more registered families, more baptisms, maybe even more ordinations. We might refine our target by measuring the percentage of families contributing to the offering, attendance counts at faith-formation activities, or the number of members who volunteer for parish ministries. It's all about keeping the Church up and running, generation after generation, we think. The goal of evangelization is to make more Catholics, right? Almost.

If we see the pews emptying out, we can reasonably guess that a failure of evangelization is part of the problem. And yes, evangelized Catholics do give more of themselves and their hard-earned cash to the work of the Church. But as we'll see ahead, persuading someone to join or become more active in a parish is not the same as evangelizing. In fact, the "head-count" way of thinking is something the Church warns against by another name: *proselytizing*.

Evangelize, Don't Proselytize

If we Catholics are hesitant at times to evangelize, some of that is due to a healthy fear: We know deep inside, even if we don't have the right words for it, that proselytizing is a grave sin. It hurts our neighbors rather than helping them. So what is the difference?

To proselytize is to treat another person as an object. Proselytizing is a form of manipulation, in which I persuade my neighbor to act in a way that suits me — in this case, by giving outward assent to a set of lifestyle decisions and theological propositions. When I proselytize, I grab good tools from the evangelization toolbox, but I use them the wrong way, with the wrong heart.

Allow me to tell a story that might shed light on the difference. When my children were young, we used to practice showing appropriate gratitude for birthday and Christmas gifts. I would find the most horrible presents ever — a smushed pinecone, a handful of gravel, an old dirty sock — and playact giving that gift as if it were the best thing ever. "Look, I got you an old dirty sock! Don't you love it?"

My children would play right back, putting on a big smile and saying, "Wow! What an interesting gift!" or "Now *that* is a surprise!" or "No one's ever gotten me one of these before! Thank you!"

The goal, consistent with the etiquette of gift giving in our culture, was to avoid that awful moment when a child receives a not-so-exciting gift from a well-meaning friend or relative and betrays a reaction that is hurtful to the giver. But was this training good, or was I just teaching my children to be fake and manipulative? Everything depends on our intentions and deeper purpose.

Here are some bad reasons and intentions:

- to make the parents look good, putting Mom and Dad's image above all else
- to greedily encourage more gift giving
- to flatter and kiss up to donors who can benefit us in other ways

- to instill in the children the idea that getting along with others and not making waves is more important than anything else

Now let's look at some good reasons and intentions:

- to show genuine appreciation for the thoughtfulness of the gift giver, making a deliberate choice to honor the person's good intentions without judging how well he or she guessed the whims of a child
- to teach the children to set aside their tastes and preferences in areas that are of no importance (Does it really matter if someone gives you a tacky sweater? So what? How does that hurt you?) and focus instead on the kindness and love at the heart of the gift giving
- to instill in the children a sense of gratitude for even the most unlikely gifts, by practicing the outward exercise of looking for the beauty and goodness in seeming disappointments, until slowly the heart catches up

In sum, a healthy approach to the gift-receiving exercise is built on the goal of loving one's neighbor and oneself through the growth of virtue.

Proselytizing focuses on externals only: getting people to show up, to say the right words, and to carry out the right actions, because it makes us look good or feel good to see measurable results. *Evangelizing* is about genuine love for our neighbor, in a way that exceeds all other loves.

Will your parish or ministry participation levels go up if you evangelize? Probably so. But evangelizing goes far, far deeper than a question of head count. Evangelization is about matchmaking.

Proclaiming the Good News

The Catholic Faith is real. It is true. It is a historical fact. God's existence and his action in our lives are not good feelings or edifying myths. God is real, and the Catholic Faith tells us the truth about our relationship with God. That truth is the "Good News," or the *kerygma*.

What is that truth?

God is Father, Son, and Holy Spirit, three Persons in one God.

God made the world: not only physical, visible things, but also spiritual, invisible things.

Original sin broke our relationship with God and with one another, ushering suffering and death into the world.

Jesus Christ, God the Son, became man and died on the cross to rescue us from our sins and restore our relationship with God. His sacrifice enables us to do what we were created to do: to live forever in heaven in perfect joy and perfect loving intimacy with God.

After his death on the cross, Jesus rose from the dead, body and soul. Then, after forty days spent teaching and commissioning his apostles, he went up to heaven, body and soul.

The Holy Spirit descended on the apostles at Pentecost, which was the founding of the Catholic Church. The Catholic Church we know today is that same Church, still guided by the Holy Spirit.

Everything we read about in the Gospels is the real, true record of the time Jesus spent on earth. It's not an allegory or a myth; it's what actually happened.

At the end of time, Christ will come again to judge the living and the dead. We will be resurrected, body and soul, either for eternal happiness in heaven or for eternal torment in hell.

And you can fill in all kinds of other details.

Kerygma, the code word that evangelists sometimes use as shorthand for this good news of Jesus Christ, comes from a Greek word that means "to proclaim, announce, or preach." It has come to mean the core message of Christianity proclaimed by the early Church, and proclaimed by us when we evangelize.

Why do I list out that message in such detail? Because when we evangelize, we're helping someone reach a goal. That goal is not mere attendance or volunteerism. We're sharing what the Good News really is: not a warm, fuzzy, comforting feeling, but rather the inescapable fact of Jesus Christ, our Messiah, the Son of God, who entered into history, died for our sins, rose from the dead, and ascended into heaven, where he sits at the right hand of the Father. Our evangelization is focused on bringing about a wholehearted embrace of the fullness of the Catholic Faith in an intimate, loving relationship with God.

> *"It is necessary to awaken again in believers a full relationship with Christ, mankind's only Savior. Only from a personal relationship with Jesus can an effective evangelization develop."*
> — Saint John Paul II, speech to bishops of southern Germany, December 4, 1992

Intimacy with Our Savior, Jesus Christ

When we evangelize, we aren't just trying to convince someone to give intellectual assent to a list of historical facts. The facts are true, and for some people, working through the evidence for those facts will be supremely helpful.

But what are those facts about? They are about the reality that the God of the universe wants each one of us to enjoy perfect intimacy and joy in a personal relationship with him.

Do you have that joy? Do you possess that intimacy?

If not, that's step one on your path to becoming an evangelist. Ultimately, our work as evangelists isn't so much about being teachers of facts and logic (though sometimes we'll do that): it's about introducing souls to the God who loves them beyond anything they can imagine. Our goal is to do our limited part in helping the people around us enter into a passionate love affair with Jesus Christ.

Love Means Seeking the Other's Highest Good

Though the flat-tire example helps us understand the importance of targeted action, human souls are not car parts. When we evangelize, we aren't trying to fix the other person. Before my conversion, it sometimes seemed as if well-meaning Christian friends viewed me as defective. If I could just get it together and see things as they did, they would be happy with me. Sometimes the kids "evangelizing" around campus would talk to me as if they didn't see me at all but saw only a target they wanted to persuade to speak the right formula. If my answers didn't fit the script, they didn't know what to do.

Evangelization is about a person to be loved, not a problem to be solved.

Let's rescue that tire analogy. What about my friends who helped me with the tire? Their number-one concern was helping *me*. They wanted me and my family to be safe, and they wanted me to be able to get on with my life and respond to all the plans God had for me that day. Their goal wasn't to turn a bad tire owner into a good tire owner; their goal was to love me and care for me.

Why do we want others to discover the beauty and joy of the Catholic Faith, the intimacy and passion of a personal relationship with God? Because that's what love is. When I love someone, I want that person to be happy. The goal of evangelization is to help people discover the one thing that is the cause of perfect happiness.

If I'm goading people into spitting out the right formula or showing up at Mass for all the right holidays, I'm not loving them; I'm trying to train them like a trick hamster.

Loving others means getting to know them, listening to them, living with them, and looking for ways, big and small, that I can serve them. That's how evangelization works.

One Soul at a Time

Thus, evangelization is not a *program*. Programming is how we make machines work for us. People are not machines. The people we evangelize are not a corps of automatons destined to fill our pews on Sundays and produce casseroles on demand for the parish potluck. We are not training a fleet of Communion-munching robots.

When we evangelize, we seek to love our neighbor as God loves him or her.

How does God love us?

One at a time.

Jesus Christ would have died for you if you were the only person on earth.

You matter. You are loved by God not for what you do or how talented you are; you are loved by God simply because you are.

God seeks you out because he wants you to know him personally. He's not hoping you'll sit in the stands with a block of fans who all blur together into a for-Jesus crowd. He wants to delight in time spent with you alone, listening to you, talking to you, comforting you, working with you.

You were made for this love. You were made to receive it from the Lord, and you were made to give it to others. God wants us to love each other with the same personal attention he gives us.

In evangelization, we discover that there is no difference between the act of love and the act of drawing others to God. To learn to evangelize is literally to learn the art of loving your neighbor. In studying that art, our first lesson is that the world is full of unique, unrepeatable persons we are called to love one by one.

When Jon and I were evangelized, each in different ways, our friends carried out for us that one life-giving act: They sought to love us each as individuals. Friends prayed not for anonymous future Christians, but for Jen or for Jon. They prayed for us by name and asked for the specific things that we each personally needed. Our friends listened to each of us. They sought to understand our individual questions and worries, and they sought to help us work through our unique difficulties.

When "evangelists" tried to treat me like some generic lump of heathen, I was repulsed. Their efforts met a dead end. When a friend broached the same topics in a genuine conversation, truly listening and responding to me, then we started getting somewhere.

Our conversions were a long, slow process. Working one soul at a time isn't the recipe for Instant Converts Now!

But that's true love. Love is in it for the long haul. Love is focused on the beloved: unique, unrepeatable, and worth every sacrifice along the way.

> **"What matters most is that you develop your personal relationship with God."**
> — Pope Benedict XVI, address to youth, New York, April 2008

Delve Deeper

Maybe you aren't sure what I'm talking about with this "personal relationship with Jesus Christ" business. You're a good Catholic, and you love being Catholic, but the idea of intimacy or friendship with God seems a little strange. Or maybe you understand it in your heart, but you can't quite put it into words.

A book that might help is *Jesus: The Story You Thought You*

Knew, by Deacon Keith Strohm (Our Sunday Visitor, 2017). This book is designed for individuals or small groups seeking to dig into the question of who God is to us and how we can find intimacy and joy in him.

For Reflection

- What is the story of your relationship with God up to this point in your life?
- How have other people helped you along the way?
- What part has God played in your relationship with him?
- What's next for you in your relationship with God, and what are some ways you might get there?

Saints for Evangelists

Blessed Bartolo Longo (October 5)

Blessed Bartolo Longo (1841–1926) was raised in a devout Catholic family in Southern Italy, but his struggling faith was no match for his virulently anti-Catholic law-school professors. He came to hate Catholicism. In the emptiness that followed, he began consulting mediums, and that foray into the occult eventually led to full-fledged satanism.

He presided as a satanic priest, consecrated himself to a demon, and publicly preached against the Christian faith. His family attempted to reason with him, and when that failed, they persisted in prayer. Eventually a Catholic professor at the university was able to confront Bartolo with how depressed and emaciated he had become. Bartolo agreed to discuss his situation with a priest, and in time he confessed his sins and returned to the Church.

He feared, however, that his sins were unforgivable. In desperation, on the verge of suicide, he turned to the Rosary. From that point forward, he dedicated himself to spiritual and corporal works of mercy, motivated by an intense desire to help others to experience the forgiving love of Jesus Christ. In proclaiming the five Luminous Mysteries, meditations on the life and ministry of Christ, Saint John Paul II was inspired by Blessed Bartolo's mystical writings.

2

Prayer

Every successful missionary effort, without exception, depends on prayer. What does it mean to have God on your team? How is the prayer of an evangelizing group of Christians distinctive?

Key Points

- Without prayer, there is no evangelization.
- We depend on God because we are his instruments — not the other way around.
- Your mission needs a prayer team.
- Those who pray for your work are the most important members of your team.
- When you want something done, ask God to do it!

Fish swim, dogs bark, Christians pray. That concept was hammered into my head when I was a newly reverted Christian, and when I looked back on my conversion, it made sense. The long years I spent barely-Catholic or squarely agnostic were punctuated by episodes of prayer, or something like it, stark moments when God reached down and reminded me he was there.

I don't have a gift for prayer. I know how to do it, and I sometimes put effort into doing it well. Too often I give the bare minimum and then later kick myself for my past stinginess when I reap the bountiful graces that come from just a little more time and attention and devotion. But I can attest that prayer is the one thing needed in every Christian mission.

If you do nothing else, pray.

Why Do We Pray?

One short Bible verse lays down the gauntlet: "Pray constantly" (1 Thes 5:17). How can this even be? Can I pray while I'm sleeping? While I'm working at my job that requires my total mental attention? How about while I'm sinning, and know it, and my life is becoming an utter train wreck?

Yes. Yes, I can pray, because to pray is to be with God.

Prayer is the opposite of hell. Eternal damnation is absolute, total, permanent separation from God. What are the things that "feel" like hell? They are the things that make us feel alone and abandoned: pain, rejection, isolation. *Despair* is that moment when we feel we have no hope. We feel we can never be worthy enough to be loved by God or man, or we feel we can never find our way out of our difficulties because we are alone against impossible odds. We weren't created to be alone, and thus despair is downright deadly.

We were created, above all, to be with God. When I pray, I am choosing to be with God — even if that means dragging him into my busyness or my wretchedness. (Not to worry: he knows the territory. You can't take him any place he has never been.)

Now, as evangelists and human beings, we can't leave our prayer life at that level. Remember when I said that our relationship with Jesus Christ is a love affair? Well, I have another love affair in my life that sheds some light on prayer — my marriage. There are times when my husband and I are just humming along, doing our thing, living more or less in touch with one another. The fact of our marriage, our love, and our intimacy with one another isn't lessened by the reality of daily life. But sometimes — indeed, daily, whenever possible — we need to connect with one another in more deliberate ways.

- We need to talk to each other about day-to-day happenings.
- We need to discuss serious issues the two of us must tackle as part of our vocations.
- We need to work through conflicts with each other.
- We need to share our hopes and dreams and aspirations with each other.
- We need to take time to explicitly show gratitude and appreciation and love for each other.
- We need to ask each other for help.
- We need to revel in the pure joy and intimacy of our marriage relationship.

Prayer does all these things, and if the marriage analogy works, it's because God has chosen marriage to be the image of his relationship with us.

Because it's *God* we're talking about, the Bridegroom of the Church, of course our prayer relationship is going to go a touch further than the time spent together between a mere human husband and wife. (My husband's a fantastic man, but he didn't create the world out of nothing, and he doesn't hold me in existence from moment to moment — though he certainly does what he can to assist.) As human beings, we *need* to adore and worship God, our Creator and Redeemer.

How Should We Pray?

I could give you some generic marriage advice, such as "take a date night" or "help your spouse with the chores," and that advice might work for many couples, but there will always be exceptions. What about the spouse who is deployed overseas? What about the spouse rendered helpless by a terrible illness? There is no single secret formula for success in marriage above and beyond the decision by both spouses to love each other completely.

So it is with prayer. I can't possibly prescribe for you the right amount or type of prayer, because I know nothing about your state in life, your vocation, and your relationship with God. Consider scheduling an appointment with your pastor or religious superior if you need help in this area.

We can, though, ask some general questions. As you think about your prayer life, or lack of prayer life, look at all those aspects of your relationship with God that we discussed in the previous section. They are all important.

Now consider the outward forms your prayer takes, whether that be during Mass; in adoration; in formal prayers, such as the Rosary and the Chaplet of Divine Mercy; in praying the Scriptures; in reciting memorized prayers; in talking with God … what *types* of time are you and God spending together?

Are you bringing to him your struggles and conflicts? Are you asking him for help? Are you expressing your gratitude? Are you and he spending time as companions? As lovers? As the human whose soul cannot rest except in the pure, exquisite intimacy of worship with your Creator?

Ask the Lord to show you where he wants you to find him and to bring into your life fellow Christians who can teach you ways to pray that answer the unmet needs of your soul.

Pray as a Team

We are created for God alone, yet we are not created to love God all alone. The communion of saints isn't an add-on; it's the reality of what it means to be human. Even if you are a consecrated hermit (yes, that's a thing, and if you are one, you already know what I'm about to say), your life is interconnected with the lives of all other humans, past, present, and future.

For that reason alone, team prayer is worth discussing. But the main reason I am going to spend a lot of time looking at *team* prayer is as much nuts-and-bolts practical as it is mystical: neglecting this essential is the number-one cause of ministry failure.

If your parish, your ministry, or your personal spiritual life is stagnating, you are probably not doing the one most important thing. In contrast, perseverance in team prayer will reap abundant fruits even when, from the outside, it appears as if nothing is happening.

Whether you are a pastor, a ministry leader, a parish volunteer, or a Christian evangelizing beyond the parish walls "all by yourself," evangelization is a team effort. Throughout this book, when I refer to your "mission" or your "mission team," don't for a moment think this applies only to certain types of Catholics who are involved in a narrow set of sponsored activities. All Catholics are called to be missionaries. All Catholics have a mission. And all Catholics have and need, whether you know it or not, a mission team.

Who's on your team?

- God
- you, whom God is allowing to play on his team
- countless others who are touching the lives of the person you are trying to reach
- the saints in heaven interceding for the one you love

You may also have some formal or informal partners you are

working with in your evangelizing efforts. They may be people who do the same work you do, or they may play other roles; they may be people you work with side by side or spiritual companions carrying out their own callings in other spheres. Ask God to show you your team. If you are feeling alone right now, ask God to put into your life team members who can encourage you and support you in whatever God is asking of you, no matter what your state in life is. Evangelization is *always* a team sport, even when it feels as if you're going solo.

What if you don't have a prayer team? You don't have a team. Before you lift a finger or say a word regarding your ministry of evangelization and discipleship, get your prayer team together and put it to work. This is true whether you view yourself as the leader or not. Who belongs on your team?

- anyone who will be involved in your ministry
- parishioners who are cheering for your ministry, even if they aren't actively involved
- Christian friends who provide support and encouragement in your efforts to be a better follower of Jesus
- that old lady you know who's really good at praying

Let's talk about that old lady. There are people you know who have a gift — a charism — for intercessory prayer. They might be young or old, male or female, physically active or absolutely incapacitated.

A *charism* is a spiritual gift that the Holy Spirit bestows on someone so that that person can carry out his or her personal mission as a follower of Jesus Christ. You can read about the spiritual gifts in the Bible (see 1 Corinthians 12 to get started). Some people have a gift for teaching or for preaching or for administration. Some people are truly gifted at the work of prayer. Ask these people to pray for your mission — not only because it will open the flood gates of God's grace on your work for him but also because praying for you is the mission of these people. When you do not invite people to pray for your work, you deprive them of the mission that is rightfully theirs.

> *"Acquire the habit of speaking to God as if you were alone with Him, familiarly and with confidence. ... Speak to him often of your business, your plans, your troubles, your fears — of everything that concerns you. Converse with him confidently and frankly; for God is not wont to speak to a soul that does not speak to him."*
> — Saint Alphonsus Liguori

How to Pray as a Team

As a lay Catholic, my mission has come in many forms. As a writer, my work is done at home, alone, with the support of colleagues who vary, based on the assignment. My team consists of Christian friends, some of whom I know locally, and others I've never met in person. Some are writers; others are not. They each support my work in accordance with their gifts, and we pray for one another in our respective vocations.

In my mission as a wife and mother, I lean on other women — both those who share my vocation and those who have markedly different vocations — for prayer support, advice, and encouragement.

As a teacher, my prayer team has taken on the work of intercession in different ways, depending on the ministry I'm working with. For several years, my teammates and I were all able to attend a weekly Mass at the same time; in a different ministry, my colleagues and I met daily to pray and study the Scriptures together before beginning the workday. I've always had back-up teams of friends and mentors who also prayed on a more informal basis.

Your options will likewise depend on many factors.

If you are able to set aside a day of the week or a night of the month for your team to gather together to pray as a group for your mission, do it! That's a good use of programming power, and in a formal group effort, it's a great way for "just a volunteer" team members to step up and take the load off the shoulders of the group leader. If you have a group of Christian friends who aren't working together, but you all share the common mission of bringing other souls to Christ, there's no reason you can't informally plan to meet during regularly scheduled parish worship to pray together for your various ministries, or schedule a time to meet privately to pray as a small group. If you are able to organize a regular Mass, Rosary, or hour of adoration on behalf of your work, make it happen!

What are some other ways you can create organized, focused prayer efforts for your mission?

- Print prayer cards that team members can use to guide their daily prayers for your work.
- Create an email list that allows team members to communicate prayer requests and respond with affirmations of prayer.
- Create an online group that uses a popular (among your team members) social media platform to communicate prayer needs.
- Write up a monthly newsletter providing news about your ministry and requesting prayers for the months ahead. If you're "just a volunteer," your story is especially important, as your friends and loved ones will delight in reading

about your work and will often be able to relate
to you as an "ordinary" Catholic more easily.

- If team members meet regularly for another
  purpose (such as carrying on the work of your
  mission), set aside time during those sessions to
  pray for the ministry and for any other needs the
  members bring to the group.

You can also activate your team members in a more organic manner. For example, you might have one prayer-team member you
meet with regularly to discuss your spiritual lives and pray for
each other, and the two of you discuss prayer requests during that
meeting. You might have another team member you speak with
after Mass, and a third you catch up with on the phone periodically. Several others might be Christians you see at work, or email
occasionally for reasons unrelated to the Faith, and when you encounter each other, you also share the latest on your respective
ministries.

How organized does your prayer team need to be? Most ministries will be a hybrid of the two approaches. Even if you have
mostly cobbled together bits and pieces of a prayer team from
disparate corners, you aren't going to pass up an opportunity for
regularly scheduled prayer. Likewise, if you have a formal team
prayer time set aside daily or weekly for your work, you aren't
going to forgo the prayers of those Christian friends who can't
easily attend.

The Hazardous Path Away from God

In one of the easiest gardening parables for a nongardener to understand, Jesus warns us of the dangers of not praying:

> Abide in me, and I in you. As the branch cannot
> bear fruit by itself, unless it abides in the vine,

neither can you, unless you abide in me. I am the vine, you are the branches. He who abides in me, and I in him, he it is that bears much fruit, for apart from me you can do nothing. If a man does not abide in me, he is cast forth as a branch and withers; and the branches are gathered, thrown into the fire and burned. If you abide in me, and my words abide in you, ask whatever you will, and it shall be done for you. (John 15:4–8)

This part of the metaphor of the vine and the branches has got to be the most in-your-face comparison in all of Scripture:

- Branch attached to living plant = alive, able to grow
- Branch cut off from living plant = dries out, dies, tossed in fire

You don't have to grow up on a farm to understand this one. And yet it's depressingly easy for us Christians to forget the spiritual reality behind this metaphor. Perhaps that's why Jesus thought that the apostles needed a good smack of common sense to help them remember.

I'm very familiar with some of the common hazards of the spiritual life that can keep us from praying as we ought.

> **"The kingdom will grow insofar as every person learns to turn to God in the intimacy of prayer as to a Father and strives to do his will."**
> — Saint John Paul II, *Redemptoris Missio*, "On the Permanent Validity of the Church's Missionary Mandate," 1990

Hazard #1: Lulled to Sleep

Much of our Jesus-work involves ordinary everyday tasks. We gravitate toward ministries that use our natural talents, so that there's rarely a sense of desperately relying on God. If you're a skilled secretary, it's unlikely that you'll feel overwhelmed with the terror of stepping out in faith and answering the phone. If you are a good administrator, you probably don't panic at the thought of God's calling you to get quotes from contractors about that routine maintenance work. When you are working within your area of giftedness, even tasks that might overwhelm the average person — public speaking, or accounting, or solving a tricky bit of repair work — won't bother you a bit. You are just doing the thing you were made to do.

Doing things that are easy for you can get pretty comfortable. At times, your work might even get downright boring. Other than praying for more vacation time, you might let God almost fall out of the picture.

Hazard #2: Too Busy to Pray

Generous people get busy. When you say yes to God's call in your life, it's easy for your schedule to get so full of the work of your ministry that prayer time gets squeezed to a minimum or even skipped altogether. "My work is my prayer!" some plead.

No. Your prayer is your prayer.

Let's be honest: If you don't love praying, you might be looking for excuses to do things other than pray.

Hazard #3: Not Actually Evangelizing

Let's go back to the secretary so boldly answering the phone at the parish office. Very few of us have that calling, but it's one we can all understand because, sooner or later, you end up needing something from that secretary!

Here's a reality that's underappreciated: For many people, the parish secretary stands in as the voice of Jesus Christ. I know we properly speak of priests as acting *in persona Christi,* and they do. But when people get up the nerve to call the parish office, they are looking for Jesus. They are calling to find out when and how they can meet God in the sacraments. Or they are calling to find out if there is a community of loving people who can befriend them on their journey toward God. Or they are calling to find out if God is present and working in this parish community the way he was working in their parish back home. It's the secretary who answers, but it's Jesus the callers are looking for.

Most of us are not the parish secretary, but all of us experience these moments when we are the face of Christ to someone we meet. When we remember that and truly understand that, our reaction is threefold:

- Thank you, Jesus, for this amazing opportunity to lead someone closer to you!
- Dear Lord, I pray that you will help this person hear your call and answer you! Help me to be your hands and feet and voice and heart in this person's life.
- Oh my goodness, I have to get this right, Lord! Help me not to screw this one up!

In our family lives, in our friendships, at work, at leisure, and when we are attending to necessary chores such as going to the dentist or picking up groceries, other people are looking up to us. They long to see in us the graciousness and love that should be a fact of human life (and too often isn't) and should be the fruit of our relationship with Jesus Christ.

That's terrifying! God himself has appointed me to be his hands and feet ... knowing full well what a bad attitude I have sometimes. Ouch. That's not something I'm going to succeed at by my own fallen, limited human powers. The only way this system is going to work — and it is God's system — is if I let God carry out through me the work that only he can do.

In other words, I must be driven to prayer as surely as a branch draws sap from a vine.

What Does the Prayer of the Evangelist Look Like?

When our mission is rooted in dependence on God, it takes on a certain character.

- We openly acknowledge that God is the one acting in our lives to orchestrate every aspect of our mission.
- We seek God's perfect will in all that we do. We dread taking even a single step that is not in accordance with God's plan for us. With God's guidance, we are willing to take any step he asks us to take.
- We recognize our need for God's help in carrying out the details of our work. We pray for our friends by name and make specific requests regarding their needs.

We aren't looking for just a general blessing — we are looking for God to take an active part in our work through his all-knowing, all-powerful, all-loving care. We know that without prayer, there can be no mission.

For Reflection

- Is prayer easy or difficult for you? What does your daily prayer life look like?
- Have you ever had a time when you got "too busy for

God"? How did that go?

- Who are some people who can pray for you? How can you be in touch with them to let them know what your prayer needs are?
- What is a realistic daily prayer routine for you at this point in your life?
- What are some things you can do to keep yourself connected to Jesus Christ in regular prayer?

Saints for Evangelists

Venerable Antonietta Meo

"Dear Jesus, tell the Holy Spirit to enlighten me with love and to fill me with his seven gifts. Dear Jesus, tell Our Lady that I love her and want to be near her. Dear Jesus, I want to tell you again how much I love you. My good Jesus, look after my spiritual father and grant him the necessary grace. Dear Jesus, look after my parents and Margherita. Your little girl sends you lots of kisses."

To be a disciple is to live for Jesus Christ. Venerable Antonietta Meo (1930–1937) is a model for all disciples in that she has no particular accomplishments to her credit other than that she wholeheartedly offered herself and her pain entirely to God. In the last years of her short life, she lost a leg to cancer, resumed school, and finally died of the metastasized cancer after a period of intense suffering. Her holiness is known to the world because she spoke freely about her love of Jesus and dictated numerous letters to the Lord, offering him her suffering, her affection, and her complete trust in his divine will.

3

Fasting

Fasting means not eating food. It is a necessary part of all missionary work. Other forms of penance can be exquisitely helpful as well, especially in cases where fasting from food is not appropriate.

Key Points

- Fasting is not optional. If you or your team is not ready to fast, you are not ready to evangelize.
- There are certain situations when you should not fast.
- The most important part of an evangelizing team are the people who offer up their suffering and penance on behalf of the missionary work.

Different Christians have different gifts, and it can be fun to sit around the table and compare notes. This one says, "I love to work with the homeless," and the next one says, "There's nothing that delights me more than spending an hour in adoration." This catechist enjoys kindergartners; that one likes teens. Is your passion directed toward visiting nursing homes, doing repairs around the parish, or flipping pancakes for that K of C breakfast? We're all different. It's a joy to see someone's eyes light up as that person explains his or her God-given way of serving the Lord.

I have never, ever, heard anyone say, "And what I really love about serving Jesus? Not eating."

The Biblical Command to Fast

"And when they had appointed elders for them in every church, with prayer and fasting, they committed them to the Lord in whom they believed" (Acts 14:23). Pull out your favorite Bible software (I like the free, online Biblegateway.com, which has multiple Catholic versions) and do a search for "fasting." The pattern is clear: In times of need, believers fast. In the Old Testament as in the New, when seeking the Lord's guidance or deliverance, fasting is part of the equation. This is true in times of great suffering, in times of repentance, in times of anticipation (such as the prophetess Anna's awaiting the coming of the Messiah), and in moments of spiritual need (such as when the apostles commissioned the first generation of deacons, priests, and bishops).

Answers from God come *after* a process of prayer, sacrifice of worldly pleasures, and spending a certain amount of time abstaining from food. That not eating thing? That's fasting.

Fasting Hurts

Our physical hunger for food is a God-given survival drive. In times of scarcity, indifference to eating would be an absolute disaster. Given this fallen world, where many people struggle daily to get food on the table, if we just didn't care whether we ate or not, it would be far too easy to give up and waste away. In wealthy societies where food is abundant, we see this drive in reverse: it's hard to turn off the part of our brain that shouts, "Quick! Food! Eat it while you can!"

Thus, the act of not eating when we are able to do so requires denying an important part of ourselves. It is difficult to fast because we must temporarily set aside a good, powerful, important aspect of human life and health.

This tells us something else about fasting: it's not simply the act of not eating due to lack of food or illness. To fast is to choose not to eat when you otherwise could.

What Happens When You Fast?

Physically speaking, in a healthy human body, what happens when you fast is that you burn stored fuel. Done prudently, it's not a big deal, as long as you don't have a medical reason that would make it dangerous for you — though you might. So consult your physician before you fast, and stay in touch with your medical team, because fasting sometimes reveals previously unknown medical conditions. More on that below!

Spiritually, quite a lot happens. The first is that you feel hungry, and you wish you could eat, and you don't. You deny yourself. This is one of the reasons that fasting for spiritual reasons is different from starvation due to lack of food or even fasting as a medical treatment. When you fast for spiritual reasons, you freely choose to give up something that physically you could take or leave, and your mind and body are shouting, "Take!" and your soul must say, "Leave."

Thus, when you fast, you are making the decision to put your service to God ahead of your service to yourself. You aren't harming yourself (see below!) any more than you harm yourself when you let the person behind you go ahead of you in line at the grocery store or let someone else be the first to open his or her gift on Christmas morning; you're just choosing to put yourself in second place.

As a result, fasting takes on some important spiritual attributes:

- You practice trusting in God.
- You grow in your ability to deny yourself.
- You learn to become a "fool for Christ" (1 Corinthians, chapter 1), denying yourself food for no "good" reason other than that it is the way God has chosen.

And finally and most importantly, we know from experience and from Scripture that fasting is one of the ways in which humans are permitted to share in the miraculous, soul-saving work of God.

What is that work? Jesus Christ, who is perfect love, chose to give himself freely for us. It is the nature of love, and thus the nature of God, to suffer and sacrifice for the one who is loved. Dying on the cross had no obvious "physical" benefit, yet it caused the single most miraculous and powerful event the world has ever seen, the opening of heaven to every soul that chooses to accept the gift of eternal salvation.

We humans, made in the image of God and called to work with and for God, are body and soul. Sometimes our spiritual work causes physical benefits, such as when prayer helps lower blood pressure. With fasting, it's the other way around: Freely chosen physical sacrifice causes spiritual work to happen.

Why is that so? How exactly does it work? Ultimately it boils down to the fact that God has made it so and has set the example himself. Fasting, for those whose state in life allows it, thus becomes, by God's design and plan, an essential part of our work of evangelization.

"Like Christ, we are all called to light, by way of the cross, for He has told us: 'If anyone wishes to come after me, let him deny himself, and take up his cross daily, and follow me,' and he shall have a treasure unfailing in heaven. ... We wish these sufferings of mind and body not only to be steps in the sufferer's ascent to his eternal fatherland, but also to contribute greatly to the expiation of others, to the return to the Church of those who unfortunately are separated from her, and to the long-desired triumph of Christianity."

— Saint John XXIII, *Ad Petri Cathedram*, "On Truth, Unity and Peace, in a Spirit of Charity," 1959

When and How Should You Fast?

Because fasting requires us to deny powerful natural instincts, it's very easy to talk ourselves out of it. We make excuses or attempt to substitute alternatives. We'll see below that there are times when you should not fast. But as a general rule: you need to pray, you need to do good works, and you need to offer up your daily struggles with an attitude of trust in God's loving mercy. All that is true and important. But you also need to fast.

The Church, in her wisdom, prescribes a minimal amount of mandatory fasting, recognizing that, in giving instructions to a billion people, personal circumstances will vary quite a bit. You should, to begin, observe the fast days set out by the Church in canon law and by your local bishop. Typically, that will be Ash Wednesday and Good Friday, plus any other days of local importance (such as, in the United States, the day of prayer and penance for the unborn). Fridays, except for those on which solemnities fall, are days of penance. Instructions on how to observe those days of fasting, or of prayer and penance, are clarified by your local bishop or your conference of bishops.

In preparing to do missionary work, whether as part of a formal effort or in your personal ministry to your acquaintances, you and your prayer team will also want to fast outside the mandatory fast days.

How do you fast? It's not complicated. You fast by not eating.

Decide to fast, and offer your time of going without food to the Lord. When you feel hungry, or start to reach mindlessly for something to put in your mouth, turn your mind to the Lord and pray, however briefly, for the intention for which you are fasting.

Keep in mind that if your body is habituated to regular caffeine consumption, you'll likely get a nasty headache and feel like a complete slug if you quit cold turkey. To avoid this, you can either choose to fast but still have that cup of coffee, or you can choose to wean yourself off caffeine before you take up fasting.

Though most (not all — see below) people can go without eating for longer than we who have always lived with abundance have come to expect, and though, for certain medical conditions, fasting from food can be beneficial, the human body cannot function without water. Stay hydrated while you fast.

Be aware that there are a number of potentially dangerous complications to avoid, even if you are robustly healthy. One of the risks of long fasts is electrolyte imbalance, which can be extremely (even fatally) serious. Likewise, there can be spiritual dangers with excessive fasting. Don't take up stringent fasting without the approval and oversight of both your spiritual director and a competent, knowledgeable physician.

Don't Hurt Yourself

It is normal to feel hungry when you are fasting, but it is not normal to feel sick or lethargic. If you are attempting to fast and you feel unwell, then eat. You can fast on a different day.

When you fast, your body uses stored fuel for energy. If your otherwise-healthy body is not used to going without food, it is going to take some adjusting for your body to become efficient at accessing stored fuel. Begin by eating just three meals a day with no snacks or beverages other than water between meals.

If you tend to feel ill if you go even a few hours without eating, then take the time to check on your health before worrying about adding fasting to your life.

There are reasons you should not fast, including certain medical conditions that make fasting dangerous. If you take medications, find out from your physician whether fasting is safe and what precautions or modifications you should make to your intended fast. See below for ideas on alternate penances if traditional forms of fasting are a bad idea.

Refrain from fasting if your physical, psychological, or spiritual situation calls for it:

- Fasting makes you feel sick.
- You have a medical condition for which fasting is contraindicated.
- You are pregnant, trying to get pregnant, or nursing.
- You are not an adult. Kids and teens need to eat, no exceptions.
- You are physically frail. Work instead on gaining or maintaining what strength you can.
- You have a history of anorexia nervosa, bulimia nervosa, or another eating disorder. Don't go back there again. There are plenty of other penances with your name on them.
- Fasting will turn you into a conceited jerk because of how superior it makes you feel.
- Your fasting would be an imposition on others.

Anytime fasting hampers your ability to live out your vocation, whether physically or spiritually, it is not something you are called to do. If you have a history of being either too rigorous or too scrupulous, obey your spiritual director.

Ordinarily, you should not plan to fast on Sundays, solemnities, or other times of feasting. Save your fasting for a different day.

As this book goes to print, fasting as a dietary or ascetic practice has become something of a fad. There are cases of group fasts in which people attempt to go for days or weeks on end without eating, often with the pressure of an expensive "retreat." These events have, not surprisingly, resulted in harm to participants. This is not how Christians fast, and it's not how any sane person fasts. Don't do these events, period.

Other Forms of Penance

Whether or not you are able to fast, other forms of penance are spiritually powerful.

What do we mean when we talk about penance? Think of the famous "giving up chocolate for Lent." When you freely choose to deprive yourself of something good, that's a form of penance. You might give up desserts, social media, your favorite drink or TV show, long hot baths — little luxuries you enjoy but can go without. When you choose to unite these sacrifices to the work of the cross, you effect a spiritual work above and beyond the work of your prayer intention alone.

As you look for ways to offer up small or large sacrifices for the good of others, it may be helpful to tie the penance to the reason you are interceding. For example, if you are praying for someone with an addiction to internet pornography, consider giving up some of your own wholesome internet time as a penance on that person's behalf. If you are praying for someone whose health requires them to follow a strict diet, in solidarity you could give up a treat that you safely enjoy but which your friend can no longer eat. This joining together of the physical act and the spiritual intention can help you remember why you are sacrificing, and it can increase the fervor of your prayer as you personally feel some of the longing or deprivation that your friend suffers. Also, let's be honest — sometimes you just need the memory link so you don't forget all about your friend in need when life gets busy and distractions pile up.

Another familiar Lenten practice is to use a period of prayer and fasting to address a specific sin. You may be struggling with an addiction or a vice that requires forgoing an unhealthy behavior. Properly speaking, it isn't penance to give up a sinful habit. You're just doing what you ought. Penance and fasting are acts of choosing not to do something that you have the legitimate right to do. Still, in overcoming a vice or habitual sin, there is tremendous spiritual work that you can use for good.

When you struggle with temptation, offer up the suffering you feel as a way of interceding for others. In the words of Saint Paul, "Now I rejoice in my sufferings for your sake, and in my flesh I complete what is lacking in Christ's afflictions for the sake of his body, that is, the church" (Col 1:24). The magnificent reality is that God wastes nothing! Even the difficulties you face in overcoming your own faults and weaknesses! When offered up for the good of others, your struggles can become genuine, miracle-producing spiritual work.

Finally, sooner or later we are all plagued with unavoidable suffering. An injury or illness might cause us pain, weakness, fatigue, depression, or loneliness. A betrayal in a relationship can leave us reeling from the emotional, social, and economic fallout. An accident or natural disaster might cause us tremendous losses. In these times, we share in Christ's suffering on the cross. Like Saint Paul, we can choose to let this suffering work for the good of the world. When we choose to offer up our suffering as a form of intercession for others, we allow God to turn evil into good and weakness into strength.

Keep It Holy

Fasting is a private action. Though there are certain times when it might be generally known that you are fasting (such as on Ash Wednesday, or if you are joining in a day of penance with others), the specifics of your penitential practices generally should not be public knowledge. We are warned by Jesus, "When you fast, do not look dismal, like the hypocrites, for they disfigure their faces that their fasting may be seen by men. Truly, I say to you, they have their reward" (Mt 6:16). For the average lay Catholic adult, the obvious time to fast privately and prudently is through meals you would ordinarily eat alone or with no one in particular.

Penance Is Powerful

"The LORD will fight for you, and you have only to be still" (Ex 14:14).

Every Christian has a missionary vocation. We are all called to work as a team called the Body of Christ to carry out the Lord's work of love. Who are the players on that team?

For any given work of evangelization or discipleship, there are those who carry out the work directly: the catechist who teaches the lesson, the volunteer who washes laundry at the shelter, the employee in a secular workplace who answers colleagues' questions about the Faith.

Then there are those who support that work through related efforts: the administrator who handles paperwork for the faith-formation program; the family that delivers laundry detergent to the shelter so that the laundry can be washed; the internet friend who has a useful link to an explanation of how to explain charitably a confusing theological topic.

Some provide wisdom and counsel: the faith-formation director who organizes training for the catechists; the mental-health counselor who can advise volunteers on how to handle confused or agitated clients; the Christian executive who has been gently evangelizing at work for decades and understands the nuances of a fraught environment.

The most important part of our team, however, are the people who devote themselves entirely to prayer and penance.

It is easy to overlook this fact. It is easy to feel that when we are too old or sick or weak to "do" anything, we can therefore do nothing.

Not so.

Humans are both body and soul, and both join together to make us capable of great work. Times of physical suffering or weakness are times when our souls have much to offer. Don't let your suffering go to waste!

It is important that we evangelizers view our work from the team perspective, no matter where we fall in the vast, interconnected, interdependent working of the Body of Christ. No missionary team is complete if it does not include the spiritual offering of those who can take up prayer, penance, or the offering of their suffering on behalf of the workers in the field.

Bringing the Team Together

You likely play more than one position on Team Body of Christ. Sometimes you are Lead Evangelist; sometimes you are Logistical Support; sometimes you are Counsel; sometimes you are the Prayer Warrior. We all have to keep our ears open to the Lord's call and our eyes open for opportunities to support one another.

If you are carrying out active works of mercy, reach out to those who can support you with prayer. If you are supporting an evangelizer through practical assistance or timely guidance, make known to others the needs of the ministry you are supporting and ask them to pray for that work.

What if you are the person whose chosen vocation or unchosen suffering puts you on the front lines of the spiritual battle through your work of prayer and penance? Let those who need you to fight for them know that you are available to carry out the miraculous work on which their ministry depends.

For Reflection

- What has your relationship with food been like over your lifetime? Do you control it, or does it control you? Are there experiences from earlier in your life that have had a lasting impact on how you eat?
- What has been your experience with fasting until now?
- Are you able to fast safely? If not, what other penances can you offer instead?
- What are the "positions" you see yourself playing on Team Body of Christ? Who are some people who can offer up their prayer, fasting, or suffering on your behalf?

Saints for Evangelists

Blessed Peter Kasui Kibe (July 1)

What would you give up in order to do God's will? Blessed Peter Kasui Kibe (1587–1639), a native of Japan from a Christian family, was deported in the expulsion of the Japanese Christians. He studied theology in Macau, but due to local opposition to ordaining non-Europeans, he had to travel to Rome to be ordained. He was able to take a ship as far as India, but from there, he had to walk the rest of the way to Rome.

Peter spent two years in Europe in formation as a Jesuit priest and then returned to the East. It was a struggle to find a ship that would take him to his native island, but he was finally able to reach Japan, where, for nine years, he ministered to Japanese Christians, who were being viciously persecuted. Eventually he was captured. He resisted all temptation to apostasize and suffered torturous martyrdom. The guards finally ran him through with a spear because he kept encouraging the other martyrs not to give up the Faith.

4

Integrity

"Integrity" means "wholeness, completeness." Integrity in evangelization means that your whole self is committed to your relationship with Jesus and your desire to lead others to him.

Key Points

- Serious sin is spiritual death to your ministry.
- We all sin. The question is: What are we going to do about it?
- Allow God's grace to work through the sacraments of healing, so that you can carry out his call for you in the work of the Church.
- Use common-sense precautions to guard against sins that tend to occur in your type of ministry.

The summer she turned fourteen, I took my daughter to the doctor for a booster shot. In the routine two-minute check-up before giving the shot, her pediatrician picked up a heart murmur. Just to be careful, she ordered an echocardiogram. Weeks later, when the low-priority patient finally got in to be seen, there on the screen was a mass in her right ventricle, bobbing in the current like a giant pool float moored to the dock of her ventricular septum.

The tumor had to come out. A surreal ten days later, an otherwise perfectly healthy kid was wheeled back to the operating room to have her sternum sawn apart, tubes stuck into a vein and artery to reroute her blood supply to a bypass machine, and her heart sliced open and stopped. Along with removing the tumor, they ended up taking a slice of healthy heart tissue, a necessary margin of safety to make sure no tumor cells were left to regrow.

My daughter's operation was a potentially deadly procedure. But leaving the tumor in place? Even deadlier.

Deadly Secrets

Serious sin is like a tumor in the heart of your life, your parish, and your diocese. It's easily hidden. Sometimes it can grow for years without being noticed, unless you have some routine checkups in place to keep an ear out for trouble. You might look perfectly healthy on the outside. And taking the painful and severe measures necessary to eliminate the problem can be downright terrifying. But if you want to evangelize, you must be the ruthless physician who refuses to leave well enough alone.

Why? Not because embezzlement will cut into your evangelization budget, though it might. Not because that affair you're having is going to become public, though it might. Not because your unchecked addiction, wrath, bitterness, envy, or sloth is going to wreck your relationships or shorten your life, though that may happen as well. It is because evangelization is, fundamentally, the sharing of hearts. Jesus has to be pumping through every vessel of your being before you can share that all-surpassing, all-sustaining love with others. You want their hearts, too, to be transformed by the life of Jesus living in them.

When you choose to let serious sin remain hidden in your soul, what you are choosing is spiritual death. Like a physician who decides that a tumor blocking blood flow in the heart is no big deal, you are no longer a person whose purpose is to keep the Blood of Christ pumping through a healthy, ever-growing Body of Christ. You are no longer an evangelizer.

Confess Your Sins

"All have sinned and fall short of the glory of God" (Rom 3:23). A physician's job isn't to sell you on the idea that your body is in perfect health. A physician's job is to help you root out the problems that are keeping your body from being as healthy as it could be.

The Church, the hospital for sinners, has the same mission for the human soul. You, as an evangelist, are a wretchedly sinful person. Integrity doesn't mean "Look at me: I never sin!" Integrity means being committed to battling your sins, through frequent examinations of conscience and confession. It means having the maturity to remove yourself from situations where the sorts of sins you struggle with could utterly sink you. It means having a balanced and realistic eye toward the weaknesses of others, knowing full well that you aren't the only sinner in the room.

Take a moment to examine your conscience:

- Would you say that you are fully on board with the Catholic Faith as outlined in authoritative documents such as the *Catechism of the Catholic Church*, or do you find yourself subtly arguing against or avoiding certain doctrines?
- Are there sins you tend to justify as being allowable because of your special circumstances or reasoning, despite knowing, by the fact that you need to hide or justify those sins, that they are contrary to the Catholic Faith?

- Are there sins you commit, perhaps habitually, despite hating those sins and wishing you didn't commit them?
- Are there sins you're almost proud of, because they represent the rejection of an opposite extreme?
- Are there sins you've given up on yourself about, because you can't seem to quit?

Having examined your conscience, what are the areas of your life where you need to make a radical change? Where do you need to keep on fighting the good fight, even though you'll probably fall into the same terrible sins over and over again?

Your sins may be relatively venial, or they may be murderous to both soul and body. Regardless, don't go it alone. Chapter 22, "One-on-One Mentoring," discusses how to find a fellow disciple who can help you in your walk with Christ; you may also need professional help. Make a plan to meet with an accountability partner, a therapist, or a spiritual director for support and assistance in the war against your weakness. If you don't already have such a person in your life, ask God to send him or her.

Meanwhile, if you aren't getting to confession regularly, how can you change that? Try to find a specific day and time that you can receive the sacrament that works with your schedule.

In between confessions, you'll need to take action to guard against sin. Having identified some of your greatest vulnerabilities, what practical steps can you take to keep yourself out of trouble? Are there people, places, or things you need to avoid? How can you make that happen?

Integrity Means Accepting Your Mission

If you are head of a ministry at any level, you have a particular responsibility. Educate yourself about the kinds of problems —

both internal and external — that typically flourish in ministries like yours, and take steps to prevent, detect, and remedy those problems.

If you are the "average Catholic" just helping out, someone with no particular authority, you don't get a see-no-evil pass. You, too, have an obligation to use your wits and common sense to keep an eye out for problems in yourself and in others.

This isn't about policies and procedures. Good policies and procedures can be lifesaving to a patient in a hospital or to a ministry of evangelization, preventing, detecting, and efficiently remedying dangers as they arise. But integrity is something more: It is your own personal and complete identification with the mission, to the point that it would be unthinkable to ignore any sign that the mission is compromised.

Without integrity, you do not have evangelization. You may have something that looks like evangelization. You may have some level of evangelization happening despite yourself. But if you are not a person whose one goal is to carry out the mission God has given you, you simply aren't an evangelist.

Ask God to help you become that person. Then you can evangelize.

> *"All Christians by the example of their lives and the witness of their word, wherever they live, have an obligation to manifest the new man which they have put on in Baptism and to reveal the power of the Holy Spirit by whom they were strengthened at Confirmation."*
>
> — CCC 2472

For Reflection

- Have you been hurt by the serious sins of someone in

Christian ministry? How did that affect your faith? What has been healing for you in overcoming that harm?

- In which areas of your life have you experienced a profound conversion and can say you've truly been rescued or healed from your sins?
- In what ways does your experience of desperately needing a Savior make you uniquely qualified to help others to learn about forgiveness, mercy, and the hope of eternal salvation?

Saints for Evangelists

Blessed Sára Salkaházi (December 27)

Blessed Sára Salkaházi (1899–1944) was a teacher, activist, journalist, social worker, and martyr. Her parents were Catholic, but Sára's faith didn't solidify until adulthood. During her work, she encountered the Sisters of Social Service, a newly formed Hungarian religious association, but her vocation to that order was heavily doubted by her would-be superiors. After a long process of personal change, doubt, conflict, and renewed persistence in answering God's call for her, she took her final vows in 1940.

As World War II progressed, Blessed Sára used her position as director of a home for young women to smuggle and hide Jews being hunted by the Nazis. At her request, her superiors permitted her to make a private vow to choose martyrdom, should it be offered to her. When the girls' home she directed was raided by the Gestapo, Sára made good on that vow, an act of self-denial that is credited with the otherwise unaccountable protection of many innocents.

5

Deprogramming

Catholics are fabulous at coming up with programs, but in order to evangelize, we have to let go of our program mentality. What are some signs that I'm confusing my parish's well-meaning activities with genuine missionary work?

Key Points

- A program is an organized, planned-out way of accomplishing a goal.
- We might use programs as part of our work, but evangelization is not a program.
- Even in working with groups, evangelization and discipleship happen one soul at a time.
- A single leader cannot have sole responsibility for evangelization, because one-on-one relationships are time intensive.

In my travels, I end up attending Mass at a dozen or so different parishes every year, and I can attest that bulletins everywhere overflow with announcements of wonderful programs. We have programs to prepare for the sacraments and programs for after the sacraments; we have programs for every age and state of life and programs for getting people of different ages into new states of life; we have programs for good Catholics, bad Catholics, not-yet-Catholics, and used-to-be-Catholics.

In talking with Catholics across the nation and around the world, there's something you can almost guarantee: mention any problem that faces the Church today, and someone will propose a program to solve it.

These programs are great. But they aren't evangelization.

What Is a Program?

A program is an organized, planned-out way of accomplishing a goal. If I have three students who want to study the Bible on Thursday nights, I gather them together, and we open the Bible and start studying. Now we have a program called Thursday Night Bible Study.

If I have ten children preparing for First Communion, twenty single seniors looking for companionship, and fifteen alcoholics chasing sobriety, the solution is obvious: sort everyone out by category and come up with a solution that allows one leader to help multiple people through the same life challenge.

The same is true on the receiving end. Whether I'm struggling with parenthood or pastoring, my chastity or my checking account, my tendency is to think, "I sure wish there was a group for people like me." I don't want to struggle alone. I want to find others who can relate to me. I want to be connected with those who are able to help me.

Programs are born of a desire to give and receive help and a need to be efficient about it.

Programs Are Great! Except When They Aren't

I teach in programs. I teach groups of parents the principles of family-centered chastity. I teach groups of tweens and teens various academic subjects. I teach groups of adults at my parish the principles of the Catholic Faith. I don't just use programs; I develop them — if you need a program, complete with logistics, staffing, and a curriculum outline, just ask me. Sometimes my brain thinks up whole programs just for my entertainment. Not kidding.

As an educator, though, I find myself frustrated by the programs I create — even when I think they're fantastic! Why? Because a program in itself cannot bring about evangelization and discipleship.

Evangelization and discipleship are about nurturing *individual* relationships with Jesus Christ. That's why, as we get into the specific techniques of evangelization and discipleship, we'll see that most of the work is done one-on-one or one-on-a-few. Whether I am the group leader or "just a member" of a group, I need to set aside my herd mentality. My mind needs to focus on each person in the group as an individual with unique needs, hopes, and fears — a person who needs to be loved for him- or herself.

> *"The salvation of souls, which must always be the supreme law in the Church, is to be kept before one's eyes."*
>
> — Code of Canon Law, canon 1752

One Soul at a Table

I was leading a Bible study one day when a newer member of the group spoke up with a series of questions. The two of us had just met, so we had no prior relationship with each other. She was confident and alert, and from the nature of her questions, it seemed that she had some real challenges concerning the Catholic Faith.

She had come to the perfect place, of course, except for one small problem: The other students in the class were looking to the leaders to provide clear, objective answers about the truth of the Catholic Faith, no fluff or confusion, and out of respect for their time, we needed to provide quick answers to questions and then move forward in the chapter.

Our new student, in contrast, was eager to discuss her doubts and explore them from different points of view. She had picked up some beliefs that aren't compatible with Catholic Christianity. And because our parish had a limited number of Bible-study instructors, there was not a more suitable class to which she could be invited. Due to the timing and the size of the class, it was unlikely that she and I would have a chance to talk afterward so I could give her the one-on-one attention she needed. There was a real risk that she'd be scared away.

What to do? I answered her questions with as much sensitivity as I could, but also clearly and unequivocally. Then I prayed like crazy. I asked some trustworthy intercessors to pray for this student: that she not be discouraged or feel singled out, and that she and I might have a chance to connect again and build a better relationship.

Our prayer was answered. She came early to the next session, and she and I had time to get to know each other. The next session's topics allowed her to share some of her experiences that were exactly what the others needed to hear. As I taught, I looked for ways to make space in the discussion for her to be affirmed and respected for what she brought to the table. We were able to continue building a relationship of mutual trust and respect that, I hoped, would bear fruit down the road.

This heart for the individual isn't only a leader's job. Every member of the study group contributed to that one-soul-at-a-time approach to welcoming our friend. Some could relate to her experiences and share relevant insights during class discussion; some could offer time or friendship outside of class; others loved her with selfless patience and prayer as they set aside their own less-pressing questions and silently interceded for her specific physical and spiritual needs. Even within the context of a group program, our thinking and our actions must always be focused on treating each soul in the room as the unique, irreplaceable treasure that he or she is.

First, Kill All the Programs?

Does deprogramming mean that, in order to evangelize, we have to get rid of all our parish programs? No, it does not. But as you read this book, allow me to challenge you to think about each aspect of evangelization and discipleship without resorting to a program mentality.

Try it. Try to think about praying for evangelization without creating a prayer program. Try to imagine building trust among non-Catholics or disaffected Catholics without coming up with some kind of special trust-building group activity. Try to imagine proclaiming the Gospel to a single person, sitting alone across the kitchen table, rather than standing at a podium, speaking to a crowd.

This is scary stuff! Programs are safe. The program structure lets me focus on measurable inputs. I contributed this class, I organized that meal, I delivered those supplies. I can point to my accomplishments and know I've done some small thing to help. Programs are comforting in the face of my limited time and energy. When I'm serving in a group or to a group, I feel as if I'm reaching more people.

When I step away from the program, I step away from my comfort zone. As a teacher, I can no longer be happy that most of my students benefited enough from the lesson; now I have to ask a different question: How can I help this student, whose needs I can't even know until we spend time listening to him or her? As a worker with the homeless, I can no longer be happy that many people received some encouragement and sustenance from my soup-kitchen meal. Now I must I ask: What about *this* man who's headed down to the bridge to sleep tonight? What about *this* woman who's in and out of abusive relationships because she can't pay the rent?

Stepping outside the program means making the decision to be Saint Simon of Cyrene. Remember, Saint Simon was the guy minding his own business, caught up in the crowd while Jesus was carrying his cross toward Cavalry. Jesus kept falling under the weight of his cross. Simon was ordered to help Jesus carry his cross the rest of the way.[*] He didn't help carry a generic group of crosses for a typical cross-carrying distance. He helped *this* man carry *this* cross at *this* time to *this* place. What started out as a horrifying ordeal for Simon became his precious act of love for the Lord.

Thank God, most of the time we are called to far less-harrowing works of mercy. But whether I am serving as part of a group or on my own, when I step outside program thinking, I make the decision to serve like Simon toward Christ, one individual to another. I'm going to look at the image of Christ in front of me and pick up this person's cross, today, right now, and walk with him or her until the Lord tells me to lay that cross down.

A Balanced Attitude toward Programs

Letting go of my program mentality doesn't mean I need to abandon programs forever and ever, amen. But for programs to work, we must always remember that programs serve individuals, not the other way around:

---

* See Mark 15:21, Matthew 27:32, or Luke 23:26–32.

- When someone doesn't "fit in" with a class or a set of program requirements, it is not the individual who is at fault. How can I, as a leader or a fellow group member, find ways to better meet the needs of that person?
- Certain aspects of evangelization and discipleship can never be accomplished with programs, because those aspects are simply too personal. How can I be sensitive to situations in which I need to carve out individual time and attention for the people around me? When I'm not the right person for the job, can I make an introduction to the right companion for this situation?
- Even when a well-designed program is a good fit for everyone involved, we still must tailor our work to every single individual in the room. No exceptions.

What! Every single person! That's right. Because evangelization and discipleship are about individual souls.

Does that sound impossible? Well, it is if you try to conduct church as usual, with a single leader responsible for being the full-service, one-stop-shop caring for dozens or hundreds of souls.

Does it seem as if your parish ministries are never sufficient to serve the people in your parish or community? From your vantage point in your family, parish, or community, does it seem as if too many people are falling through the cracks? Does it feel as if you have been hitting a wall in your efforts at evangelization and discipleship because you just can't seem to meet everyone's needs?

I have some good news: That wall is real.

The work of evangelization and discipleship was never meant to rest on the shoulders of a few leaders carrying out a handful of carefully orchestrated ministries. Unchain yourself from the futile quest for the perfect program. Evangelization and discipleship are not programs and never will be.

For Reflection

- What program have you had a good experience with? What made it work so well for you?
- When have you felt like the square peg in a round hole, expected to attend a program that just wasn't a good fit for your needs?
- When did someone give you individual help and attention? How did that happen? How did it feel?
- When have you helped someone one-on-one without going through any formal channels? Think of a time when you realized someone needed something, and you decided to stop and help that person on your own.

Saints for Evangelists
Blessed Joseph Gérard (May 29)
Blessed Joseph Gérard (1831–1914) joined the Missionary Oblates of Mary Immaculate and was sent to southern Africa to become a missionary priest, where his gift for learning languages proved valuable. After a brief, discouraging time among the Zulu, he was sent to establish a mission community in Lesotho. He received the king of Lesotho's permission to do so and earned the king's respect when he did not leave Lesotho when the region was engulfed in war.

Despite his ability to speak the local language and his strong relationship with the king, his missionary work did not achieve quick results. It took two years before he saw a single conversion. After fifteen years of evangelizing, there were only seven hundred Catholics in the country. Nonetheless he persisted, valuing faithfulness to the Lord's missionary call over numerical results, focusing on each individual soul who came into his care. He continued establishing missions and serving the community in Lesotho for the remainder of his life, and he is remembered in particular for his willingness to set out on long journeys in any weather to bring the Blessed Sacrament to the sick and the elderly.

6

Listening

When we evangelize, we help people meet God. Just as a doctor listens to a patient, we must learn to listen for clues about what is going on in someone's life and how that person's friendship with God is progressing.

Key Points

- Attentive listening is an act of love.
- Listening is a skill we need to practice.
- Gentle, attentive listening uncovers the deeper story.

When you pray, do you know what God does? He listens to you. In fact, he doesn't listen to you only when you are talking to him. He is attentive to you in every moment of your existence. He is attentive to your fears, your suffering, your hopes, and your frustrations. He is attentive to the state of your body, down to the inner workings of each cell and each ion in each molecule that passes from one cell to another — and then further down than that.

Loving another person requires knowing that person, and getting to know that person requires the attention of our minds and hearts. In fact, to love someone is to pay attention to him or her.

When we are trying to evangelize, though, sometimes we forget to listen. We forget that evangelization is the act of loving another person, and instead we go into fix-it mode. The impulse is good; helping people solve their problems can be an act of mercy. But we have to make sure we have listened long enough and well enough — that we have been truly attentive — so that our response is one of authentic love.

What Does Good Listening Look Like?

- We let the other person "dominate" the discussion. It's the other person's turn to talk and our turn to listen.
- We focus our mind on truly hearing what the person has to say, rather than thinking about our own ideas or what we will say next.
- We ask questions for clarity or to go deeper, not in order to steer the conversation.
- We allow the person to explore difficult or uncomfortable topics.
- We acknowledge the person's point of view, even if we don't agree with it.
- We ask questions to confirm that we've understood correctly.

Listening Is a Skill

You can improve your listening skills through practice. Pick someone you know — a family member, a friend at church, a colleague — and set a timer for five minutes. During that five minutes, have that person talk while you practice listening attentively. If you like, switch roles and do a second round of five minutes.

You can also practice on the sly. When you sit down to a meal with a friend or a family member, make the decision secretly that today you are going to let the other person do all the talking. If the person tries to steer the conversation your way, make a short, friendly answer and then ask another question to get him or her going.

Some people are better conversationalists than others, and some people are better natural listeners than others. The best listener I know is my daughter's pediatrician (the one who picked up on that heart tumor). In order to do her job well, she has to listen carefully to her patients. Years of practice have perfected her skill as a listener.

When the Words Hurt

Often in evangelization encounters, listening involves hearing painful attacks on all you hold dear. For someone who loves God and loves the Catholic Faith, it's easy to get defensive!

Remember, if the other person were living in perfect union with Jesus Christ in the Catholic Faith, there would be no need to evangelize. By definition, when you are evangelizing, you are encountering someone who still has obstacles to total faith.

Likewise, when it comes to discipleship, by definition we are referring to someone who is still on the path to Christian maturity. A disciple is someone who has had a profound encounter with Christ and made the decision to follow him and is now learning how to do that. ("Discipleship" can refer to the act of being a disciple of Christ, and it can also refer to the process of helping another Christian or of being helped in the process of growing in Christian maturity.) It's a lifelong quest, and all of us disciples have areas where our faith is still vulnerable. Thus, though we will look at examples of evangelizing conversations, the same skills are useful for discipleship.

> **"The missionary task implies a respectful dialogue with those who do not yet accept the Gospel. Believers can profit from this dialogue by learning to appreciate better 'those elements of truth and grace which are found among peoples, and which are, as it were, a secret presence of God.' "**
>
> — CCC 856

Bad Listening versus Better Listening

You don't need to live in terror of accidentally listening wrong. We all sometimes slip up and say the wrong thing. Sometimes even the "right" response won't guarantee sunshine and roses. Still, we can watch out for some typical listening mistakes.

Here's a common example of listening gone bad, followed by some better possible responses. You're having a conversation with a new acquaintance, and hear this: "I never felt I really knew Jesus when I was Catholic. I didn't hear the Gospel until I started attending Faith & Grace down the street."

Some thoughtless, dismissive answers might be:

- "Well, I don't know why not. Jesus is present at every Mass!"
- "You're just feeling the emotions of the rock band they have on Sunday mornings."
- "If you were serious about your faith, you wouldn't be so swayed by your emotions."

I can guarantee none of those would be helpful to the soul you're talking to. If we've been listening attentively, a better answer might be one of these:

- "Can you tell me a little more about what helped you hear the Gospel at F&G?"
- "Do you have any ideas why you had such a hard time hearing the Gospel at your home parish?"
- "Looking back, what things would you say are similar between your home parish and F&G, and what things do you think are different?"
- "I'd love to hear more about your relationship with God now."

And, of course, another option is simply to keep your mouth shut and let the speaker fill the silence with more information.

Attentive, listening answers aren't dismissive, don't make uncharitable assumptions about the speaker's motivations, and don't shut down communication.

Listening attentively means looking for ways to get the speaker to open up more.

Listening for Implications

As we are listening, we don't want to jump to conclusions about the person's motivations and inner feelings. We can, however, listen for clues about the deeper story.

For instance, suppose someone tells you "I could never believe in a God who allows such horrible things to happen in the world."

What might be the context behind that statement? The person might really be saying:

- "I am really upset by the suffering I see all around me."
- "I am grieving a particular terrible thing that happened to me."
- "I know deep inside that God is supposed to love us, but I don't know how to reconcile that with the problem of evil."

- "I feel so helpless. It seems as if nothing I can do will make a difference for good."
- "My life is falling apart right now, and I wish someone, anyone, would come to my aid."

Or, take the statement "Church people are hypocrites. I want nothing to do with them."

Some possible deeper stories could be:

- "My family experienced betrayal at the church we belonged to before."
- "I've seen terrible stories in the news about something that happened at a church, and I just can't extend any trust right now."
- "My Christian friends don't seem any different from anyone else. Why bother?"
- "I went for help to a local church, and they turned me away. I'm still really hurting from that."
- "Can you help me? This is my way of inviting you into my life, because I really need help right now."

Here's another common declaration: "I'm very spiritual. I feel more connected to God in other places than at church."

The real story might be more along the lines of:

- "Yes! I want to talk about spiritual things. I'm just not ready to commit to a particular religion right now."
- "I feel a deep longing to be closer to God, but I'm confused by the conflicting claims of so many religions."
- "Even though I was very hurt by my past experiences with church, I still really want to be with God."
- "I didn't grow up knowing anything about Christianity. This is the best I've got right now."

- "It seems as if missionaries all just want to fix me, but I don't feel broken. How are you any different?"

How do you find out what the deeper story is behind any statement?

By asking gentle questions and allowing lots of time for answers. It's okay if the conversation doesn't move in a straight line or is carried on in spurts over time. Pick up the thread next time, and keep on listening.

For Reflection

- In your life, how do you feel when someone doesn't take you seriously? How do you feel when you are interrupted, ignored, or told what you think?
- Who do you know who is a strong listener?
- When has someone listened patiently to you, so that you felt, for once, as if there was someone who understood what you were experiencing?
- Have you tried active listening exercises? How did it go? What are your strengths and weaknesses as a listener?

Saints for Evangelists

Saint John de Britto (February 4)

Saint John de Britto (João de Brito in Portuguese, and also known by his Tamil name, Arul Anandar) was a Jesuit missionary who traveled to the missions of Madurai in southern India in 1673. The Madurai mission was known for its efforts to establish a Catholic mission as free as possible from European influence. The saint sought to eat, dress, and live the way his neighbors did. More profoundly, he sought to see the world from the point of view of those he was ministering to and thus to teach the Catholic Faith in ways that would make sense to those he was evangelizing. He was martyred in 1693, and the site of his martyrdom remains a popular pilgrimage site to this day.

Part 2

How to Evangelize

Our second unit is where we gather knowledge and skills that can serve us in the work of evangelization from start to finish. We'll begin in **chapters 7** and **8** by learning some ways to think about the process of becoming Christian and the mental obstacles that can confuse our efforts to understand where someone's spiritual struggle lies.

Next, we'll delve into four areas where Catholics are already comfortable evangelizing: **The Corporal Works of Mercy (chapter 9)**; **The Power of Beauty (chapter 10),** which applies the "Little Way" of Saint Thérèse to our lives as evangelists; **The Liturgy Link (chapter 11)**; and **The Role of Apologetics (chapter 12)**. We'll see what Catholics are already doing well and learn about the limits, pitfalls, and additional skills we need to master in each of these fields of evangelization.

Ready to be pushed outside your comfort zone? **Workplace Missionaries (chapter 13)** and **Street Evangelization (chapter 14)** will teach you how to use skills discussed in previous chapters in order to bring the Gospel to people who will otherwise never hear it.

What do we have to offer those we encounter in the mission field? **Hospitality (chapter 15)**, **Crafting Parish Events (chapter 16)**, and **Retreats (chapter 17)** walk us in sequence through ways to make our homes and our parishes places to meet Jesus Christ and grow closer to him.

Finally, we need to learn how to help someone make the leap into discipleship. In **Proclaiming the Kingdom (chapter 18)** and **The Ask (chapter 19)**, we'll learn to use our words to extend the invitation to become a follower of Jesus Christ in the Catholic Faith. **Companions on a Long Walk (chapter 20)** examines the challenge of pastoral accompaniment when the decision to follow Christ isn't easy.

What's next for the new Catholic? **Part 3, Discipleship.**

7

The Five Thresholds

What are we listening for? We are listening to understand the other, and to figure out how to be truly helpful. An important set of concepts that can help us understand where someone is in his or her relationship with God is a framework called the "thresholds of conversion."

Key Points

- The five thresholds of conversion are stages on the path toward faith in Jesus Christ.
- If we listen closely, we will often find that people are not nearly as far along the path as we might have guessed.
- We are not mechanics trying to fix a broken car. Listening as an act of love sets the stage for evangelization and discipleship as an outgrowth of that love.

Evangelization is as old as Jesus Christ. The human heart is no different today from what it was when Our Lord walked the earth. When we speak of the "New Evangelization," we don't mean that we are promoting some new Gospel. We mean that society and culture are different from generation to generation, and we must look to the spiritual needs of the people in front of us right now.

In trying to get a firm grip on how to evangelize today, it is useful to know some concepts that will help us better understand what our neighbors may be thinking and feeling. First, we will look at the idea of "thresholds of conversion." In the next chapter we'll talk about something called Moralistic Therapeutic Deism. We'll see what the limits of these ideas are and also how we can use them fruitfully.

The Five Thresholds of Conversion

In the seminal work *Forming Intentional Disciples*, author and evangelist Sherry Weddell lays out five thresholds of conversion, or stages on the path to discipleship. We'll look at each in turn.

Trust

Imagine that you are taming a feral cat. You found the poor creature living under your porch, and you set out food for it. At first, it didn't dare come near. Eventually hunger overcame terror, and the starving animal developed just enough courage to sneak up at night and steal a few bites while looking around furtively, dashing off at the least sound.

Is your cat tame yet? Definitely not.

Fast-forward a few weeks. The cat has learned that the food bowl is a safe place. It now comes up in daylight, eats contentedly, and goes back to its lair under the porch.

Is the cat tame? No, but it has reached an initial level of *trust*.

People are not cats, and evangelization is not about turning a free creature into a house pet, heaven forbid! But the visual of the cat that bolts in terror gives us an idea of how people who have no trust in the Catholic Faith feel.

- Perhaps they have grown up in a religion that is staunchly anti-Catholic and have been told all sorts of wicked myths about the Church. (I have a friend who grew up hearing stories about how the bishop's miter is worn to hide the horns on his head; the modern counterparts are accusations that the church hates women and is anti-science.)
- Perhaps they have no trust because they have seen the true accounts in the news of clergy who lie, steal, molest, and blackmail — scandals that touch every level of the hierarchy.
- Perhaps they were raised in a Catholic home but were victims of abuse at church or at a parish school.

There are a multitude of reasons why someone might have a powerful fear of getting involved in anything to do with the Catholic Faith. When we talk about someone reaching the threshold of *trust*, we don't mean that the person is ready to get baptized and start singing in the choir. We do mean that the person no longer gets a knot in the pit of his or her stomach when he or she thinks of the Catholic Faith. The person no longer hates or dreads. He or she has enough connection to the Faith to be willing to come up onto the metaphorical porch of the Church. People at the threshhold of *trust* are willing to have Catholic friends, to be around Catholic conversation, to have some things to do with some aspects of Catholicism — and indeed, they might be quite at home spending time in the church if they have reached an advanced state of trust.

Many people who come to Mass and participate in parish life

are, in fact, only at the stage of trust — even if they are lifelong Catholics.

How do we build a bridge of trust? First of all, by proving ourselves trustworthy!

People may already have a bridge of trust because they have family who are Catholic. A Catholic friend at work or school might have proven over time that Catholics are decent, loving people. One acquaintance shared how touched she was by the tenderness of the treatment she received at a Catholic hospital. Several non-Catholic parents at my daughter's parish school said they initially didn't even know that non-Catholics could attend a Catholic school, but now that their children have been attending, they wouldn't go anywhere else. Those are all bridges of trust.

> *"Many people perceive Christianity as*
> *something institutional — rather than as an*
> *encounter with Christ — which explains why*
> *they don't see it as a source of joy."*
> — Pope Benedict XVI, May 2004

Curiosity

People are not cats, but we'll continue with the metaphor. Imagine that your furry friend has gotten comfortable lounging on the patio furniture and will even let you come and give it a scratch behind the ears. That's an advanced stage of trust. Now the cat begins exploring. You leave the front door open, and the creature slips into the house and pokes around. Cats are notoriously curious, after all.

One winter morning, you realize that your visiting cat has made itself a bed on a shelf in your garage, safe from the chill outside. You start to imagine it's "your" cat now.

It is similar with the Faith: People at the *curiosity* stage poke their noses around a bit and may even have made a home for themselves in the Church. They like to talk about the Catholic Faith. They may find elements of Catholicism to be a positive addition to their lives. Someone who is curious may be active in parish ministry and regularly attending Bible study. And yet, if we listened intently, we'd hear that these curious parishioners are still at only a very early stage on the path of evangelization and discipleship.

Curiosity can be a frustrating stage in evangelization because it is easy to expect too much or too little. For a new evangelist, this is a comfortable stage, because the ordinary practice of Christian friendliness is just right in relationships with those who are curious. What we need to guard against is thinking that curiosity is conversion and that our is work is done. We mustn't allow ourselves or those we love to settle for a lifetime spent living on that shelf in the spiritual garage.

Openness

Those who are *open* to the Gospel have not yet made a decision to follow Jesus Christ in his Church, but they are willing to consider doing so. They feel a tug toward the Lord, but they may not know what questions to ask or how to find the answers.

For someone who is not Catholic, *openness* might sound like this: "I could imagine myself being Catholic. I don't know if it's what I want to do, but I'm willing to consider it."

For someone who is already Catholic, perhaps even quite active in the church, expressions of openness might include:

- "I don't really understand why the Church teaches what it does about that difficult issue, but I'm interested in learning more."
- "Sometimes I wonder if God is calling me to something more. Does that sound crazy?"
- "You know how Mother Teresa was so close to

God and so committed to serving other people?
I sometimes think about that. What would it be
like to be even half that excited about serving
God and other people?"

- "I've been reading the Bible a lot lately. I think
there's something really special there."
- "Lately I've been thinking about my life and trying to figure out what to do next."

When evangelizing someone who is open to a relationship with
Jesus Christ but not yet seeking, we want to provide support and
gentle guidance, but without overwhelming the person.

Seeking

Before our conversions, my husband and I went through a couple
of rounds of looking for churches. I would say that during round
two, we were *open*. We were looking at Christian churches specifically, and we were visiting and "trying them on." Could I fit in
here? Is this someplace I'd like to be every Sunday?

One Sunday we found a nondenominational congregation
that felt right. We felt God's presence in the worship service and
the sermon and the prayer of that group of Christians. It was ex-
citing!

We came back every Sunday. We got involved. We wanted to
learn everything about God that we could. We had questions that
needed answers. We had begun *seeking*.

If we were to verbalize the inner life of a *seeker*, we might
hear:

- "I need to know if the Catholic Faith is true."
- "I'm looking for evidence that Jesus is real."
- "Teach me more about how to pray. I need to get
to know God better."

- "I sense that God is calling me, and I need to know what that means."
- "I don't understand this difficult aspect of the Faith, and it's really important to me that I figure it out."
- "This all just feels so right. I feel as if this is something I need to do."

Because the inner life is private, seeking might never be verbalized in these ways. Someone who is seeking God is experiencing emotions and ideas that he or she may have never put into words before. It is also common for someone in a highly secular culture to feel uncomfortable about the fact that he or she is actively seeking God. There may be pressure to downplay his or her interest in religious questions and to pretend that it's strictly a cultural or pragmatic choice. Conversely, in a Bible-Belt culture or an intentional community of practicing Catholics, the seeker may feel pressure to pretend already to be a fully, firmly committed Christian and may hesitate to reveal doubts or questions that are the mark of someone who hasn't yet joined the club. The seeker converting from a non-Catholic faith may have to overcome anti-Catholic stigmas; the seeker who is a lifelong Catholic may feel ashamed at realizing how much he or she has failed to understand of all that Catholic stuff.

As evangelists, we can overcome these challenges by upping our listening game and by offering sensitive, nonthreatening invitations to the Faith. Keep in mind that our goal here isn't to diagnose a problem and carry out a repair job. The seeker is not a problem to be solved but a person to be loved. Rather than worrying about exactly where someone falls on the path of the five thresholds, ask the Holy Spirit to show you ways to love this person more completely.

We can create a seeker-friendly emotional climate by avoiding anything that smacks of triumphalism. Be open about the fact that you yourself had questions and still have them; you had struggles and still have them. This doesn't mean there are no answers. It means that the answer of the Gospel turns our lives upside down and that our quest to follow Jesus Christ will always require us to challenge the comfortable status quo.

If you find that the sin of pride causes you to be more arrogant than evangelical, pray the Litany of Humility as often as you can bring yourself to rise to that challenge. *Seeking* is a very humbling stage, and the best way to accompany someone caught up in a humility storm is to get down on your knees and shuffle along in humility with that person.

Above all, remember that the Person your friend is seeking is not you. Seeking is about a conversation between your friend and the Holy Spirit. If we evangelists are matchmakers, it is God who is the divine Lover, courting his beloved.

Intentional Discipleship

A disciple has made the conscious, firm decision to drop everything and become a full-fledged follower of Jesus Christ. A disciple has said "I do" to God.

In ministry, we sometimes refer to this as "dropping the nets," a reference to the way Jesus called Andrew and Simon, James and John, and these four fishermen left their boats and nets at the shore and became his disciples.

If you back up to the first chapter of the Gospel of John, you'll see that the call of Simon Peter and his workmates doesn't come out of nowhere. Andrew, the brother of Simon Peter, and "another disciple" — probably the apostle John — have been disciples of John the Baptist. One day, those two are with John the Baptist when Jesus walks by. John points out Jesus and says, "Behold! The Lamb of God." The two disciples go and follow Jesus, there are questions and answers, and Jesus invites them to come to the place where he is staying. At this point they are actively and intensely seeking, but have not yet dropped the nets.

Later in the afternoon, after spending time with Jesus, Andrew goes and finds his brother Simon and tells him they've found the Messiah, and Simon goes and meets Jesus. Jesus foretells that Simon will be called Cephas (Rock), from which we get the name Peter (from the Greek word for stone).

But note well that they still haven't dropped the nets.

The two pairs of brothers, Peter and Andrew, James and John, won't have that dropping-the-nets moment until after John the Baptist is arrested. In the Gospel of Mark, chapter 1, we see that it is only after the four have seen the cost of discipleship in John the Baptist's arrest, and have had some time to consider whether they want to go back to their old life, that Jesus calls them to leave everything.

Reaching the point of discipleship is a process. The four fishermen spent a long time seeking Jesus and getting to know him before they received their ultimate call. So it is for us today.

That action of answering the call to be a disciple can happen in a clearly defined moment, as it did for me and for Simon Peter. It can also happen more subtly, as it did for my husband. One day you look around and realize you aren't fishing anymore: You're out on a hillside in Judea, and you've left your old life behind without even noticing it.

> *"It is God's will that we have true delight with him in our salvation, and in that he wishes us to be mightily comforted and strengthened, and thus he wills that with his grace our soul be happily engaged."*
>
> — Blessed Julian of Norwich, Revelations of Divine Love

Comparing the Thresholds

One of our challenges as evangelists is making sense of where someone is on the thresholds. It is very easy to assume that someone is further along than he or she is. Let's look at some possible benchmarks, acknowledging that these are oversimplifications. People are complex, and our relationship with God cannot be boiled down to one stage or another. As with any relationship, it's not about a straight line toward perfect intimacy. You may grow closer to or further away from your best friend or your spouse, and in the same way, people move closer to and further away from God.

Still, we can at least try to get an idea of what it looks like as someone is growing closer to God in various contexts.

	Bible Study	Prayer	Christian Service
No trust	The Bible is a bunch of myths and fairy tales.	Prayer is just talking to the ceiling.	Catholics are hypocrites at best. I want nothing to do with them.
Trust	I imagine there's something to be learned from the Bible.	People get something of value out of prayer.	Catholics do some good things in the world, and I like that. I like being part of it.

Curiosity	Here's an interesting Bible fact.	Isn't it interesting how people from different cultures pray? I enjoy learning about that.	Isn't it great how many religious orders there are serving the poor around the world? That's pretty neat!
Openness	It's possible that God has something to say to me in the Bible.	If God wanted to speak to me in prayer, I'd be okay with that.	If God called me to be the next Mother Teresa, I'd like to think I'd say yes.
Seeking	I need to understand what the Bible is all about.	I have been praying that God will answer me. I want to know him.	I need to know what God wants me to do with my life.
Discipleship	The Bible is my guide and my go-to. It tells me how to live. I pray the Bible daily.	God is my constant companion. I turn to him in prayer as my source of wisdom, companionship, and help in everything I do.	Every day, I seek to know what God wants of me, because serving him by answering his call for me is my one purpose in life.

Threshold Conversations

Whether someone is starting from a complete lack of affiliation with the Catholic Faith or has been born and raised in the Church, sacramental milestones or parish-participation levels are not an accurate gauge of where someone is on the path toward discipleship. A *threshold conversation* is an act of intense, nonjudgmental listening that allows us to learn more about someone's relationship with God.

We say to that person, "Tell me about your relationship with God up until this point in your life."

As we listen, we ask follow-up questions to get a clearer picture. One of the rules is: Never accept a label in place of a story.

If someone says, "I'm basically agnostic right now," then, as listeners, we would reply, "Can you tell me what you mean when you say you're agnostic?"

If someone says, "I'm a very devoted Catholic," we might ask, "Tell me what devotion looks like in your life," or "Explain to me how that affects your relationship with God."

Why do we listen? Threshold conversations serve three main purposes.

1. Listening is an act of love. It is an act of taking an interest in someone else, giving up our time and our right to reply.
2. We can be a sounding board for someone trying to figure out his or her relationship with God. In asking questions that help us understand the speaker better, we also help the speaker understand himself or herself better.
3. And finally, unless we have an approximate idea of where someone is in his or her relationship with God, we really don't know which evangelizing actions might help.

When and How to Have a Threshold Conversation

Keep firmly in mind that the models and tools described in this chapter and elsewhere in the book are simplifications. They are frameworks that can be helpful in the proper perspective, but we are speaking here not of a motor in the hands of a mechanic but of the mysteries of the human heart.

To help understand the distinction, recall that the Lord chose marriage as the symbol of his relationship with the Church. As a parent, teacher, and chastity educator, it's my job at times to discuss with young people how the vocation to the married life is answered. I might speak of stages in dating or in the intimacy of a romantic relationship headed toward marriage. And yet when you ask married couples to tell the story of how they met and fell in love, it becomes clear that very few people fit some generic model of "how to meet your spouse."

So it is with the five thresholds. Two unmarried persons who are considering dating, are actively dating, or are preparing for marriage may at times have a "state of the relationship" conversation, in which they attempt to pinpoint where they stand right now and what might be next. Sometimes the answer might be "It's complicated" or "It's hard to describe." That's okay. We don't have to force human hearts into rigid procedures, so long as we proceed with gentleness and authentic love.

As with a dating couple, there might be a situation when a "state of the relationship" conversation concerning God — a formal threshold conversation — is just what is needed. If you are involved in a parish or community evangelization initiative, it might be appropriate to include threshold conversations as a specific, preplanned part of your ministry's work, just as marriage-prep programs may include preplanned moments when engaged couples will step aside and discuss, privately and nonjudgmentally, important issues to consider before their wedding. This can work if:

- **The threshold listeners are adequately trained in the art of listening.** Make sure that anyone involved in a formalized listening ministry has had many opportunities to practice and that members of the listening team are not prone to getting argumentative or falling into fix-it mode. The charisms (spiritual gifts) of listening ministers can be quite different from the charisms of some preachers, teachers, and apologists.

- **The ministry scrupulously avoids anything at all that smacks of proselytizing.** It is impossible to speak honestly and openly about one's inmost loves and fears and vulnerabilities if "giving the right answer" is necessary in order to receive some sought-after assistance or status in the community. Though we think of the corporal works of mercy as being most likely to fall into proselytizing (I have to say I love Jesus in order to get that winter coat from the parish clothing closet), the most common situation in my experience where people feel pressured to give lip service to the Faith is in preparation for the sacraments of initiation (matrimony is a close second).

- **Confidences are kept.** In the classroom I often ask students very explicitly not to share with the group anything that they don't want discussed by everyone everywhere. Gossip is a vicious and untameable beast. Listeners must be absolutely trustworthy guardians of privacy.

Most often, though, many small, informal threshold conversations will occur throughout the long, slow, soul-to-soul process of forming deep, loving, personal friendships. Your friend will share a thought here, a question there, a bit of backstory another time. You may feel prompted by the Holy Spirit to ask a gentle, nonthreatening question at an opportune moment, and the floodgates open.

Often the opportunity will come unbidden. I can think of several times when someone specifically came to me requesting what, in retrospect, would have been a prime listening-ministry moment, if only I had known how to shut up and listen for a change instead of being so eager to have all the answers. When approached by a friend, a family member, a parishioner, a colleague, or a complete stranger, you can do worse than to pray, "Lord, give me the words of your love that this person needs right now, and ears to hear this person's cry for you."

For Reflection

- Have you ever heard of the thresholds of conversion idea? How would you explain each of the thresholds in your own words?

- Are there are other ways you prefer to describe the spiritual changes that happen as people grow closer to God? How would you match up your preferred way of describing conversion with each of the stages in the thresholds model?

- Using the five thresholds as a thinking tool, where do you think you are, personally, along the thresholds of conversion? It may be helpful to partner with a friend and take turns talking about your relationships with God up until this time in your lives.

- When has someone come to you wanting to share a spiritual idea or question? As you remember that time, in what ways were you a strong listener? In what ways might you listen more attentively if you had that opportunity now?

Saints for Evangelists

Servant of God Elisabeth Leseur

Servant of God Elisabeth Leseur (1866–1914) is a study in the difference between Catholic identity and the conversion of a disciple. Raised in an affluent French Catholic home, she was shocked to learn shortly before their wedding that her future husband, Felix, was no longer practicing the Faith. Theirs was a loving marriage, but under the influence of Felix's antipathy to the Christian faith and the couple's ardently secular social circle, Elisabeth abandoned the Faith as well.

The same way she left the Faith, she would return to it, in a profound reconversion. A notable scholar of the day had written a life of Jesus, arguing against the Lord's divinity, and Elisabeth found herself studying the Bible and Catholic writings in order to refute its main points. From then on, her spirituality exemplified Saint Thérèse's Little Way, as applied to a wealthy homemaker dealing with the demands of marriage, social life, and painful illness. She undertook the evangelization of her husband and their friends through an intentional path of prayer, small acts of self-denial, and seeking to understand the other. Through her intercession and example, her husband converted after her death and was later ordained to the priesthood.

8

Moralistic Therapeutic Deism

The same word or phrase can mean different things to different people. In this chapter, we'll take a look at a common set of religious beliefs that affect how people relate to God and how they approach difficult theological and moral questions, even when they express themselves in terms that are familiar to Catholics.

Key Points

- "Moralistic Therapeutic Deism" is a name given to the predominant theological viewpoint in American culture.
- Differing beliefs about suffering, human happiness, and eternal life can create significant disagreements about how to handle difficult moral issues.
- Christian vocabulary is frequently used by people who identify as Catholic but whose beliefs are more deist than Christian.

- Being alert to important theological and philosophical differences can help us evangelize more effectively.

The phrase Moralistic Therapeutic Deism (MTD) was coined in *Soul Searching: The Religious and Spiritual Lives of American Teenagers*, by sociologists Christian Smith and Melinda Lundquist Denton. It is useful to be aware of MTD because it is a common spiritual worldview today. People we meet may use Christian words to describe their faith, but when we listen closely, we begin to realize they are still struggling to understand what Christianity is about.

As described by Christian Smith in his 2005 Princeton lecture, "On 'Moralistic Therapeutic Deism' as U.S. Teenagers' Actual, Tacit, De Facto Religious Faith," there are five tenets of MTD. We're going to work through this concept back to front, so you can see how the ideas build on each other.

Deism means a general belief that God exists. In the MTD worldview:

1. God the creator exists and watches over life on earth.
2. God does not need to be involved in our lives, however, except when needed to help solve a problem.

Therapeutic refers to the way God helps us, intervening to solve our problems, because:

3. Our main goal in life is to be happy and to feel good about ourselves.

Moralistic means having to do with good and evil. Thus:

4. God wants people to be good to one another.
5. Good people go to heaven when they die.

You can see some clear similarities with Christianity: There is a God. God does want to help us. God does want us to be good. God does want us to go to heaven after we die. All this is true.

But can you see the differences from Christianity?

Even if you have absolutely given your life entirely to Jesus Christ as a Catholic, you may have a hard time explaining how MTD differs from your Catholic Faith.

Key Differences between MTD and Catholicism
Thanks to our Catholic Faith, we know some specifics about this God who created the world and about how he interacts with us.

- We can know the existence of God and some of his attributes (eternal, all-powerful, all-good) from reason and observation alone. Divine revelation — God's telling us about himself and showing himself to us — helps us to know that God is a Trinity of Persons. Divine revelation also reveals more about the workings of the Father, the Son, and the Holy Spirit in human history.
- We know that God wants to be intimately involved in every aspect of our lives. He is present to us in the sacraments in a particular way. He loves us with self-sacrificing love.
- We know that we need a Redeemer. God wants us to be good, and yet we sin. We are aware of how terribly even "good" people sin sometimes. We know that Jesus Christ died for our sins,

and only through his saving power can we go to heaven.

- We know that we live in a fallen world, and because of this, we may experience terrible, unavoidable suffering. This present life isn't the whole picture.

- We know that our main goal in life isn't to maximize our present happiness but to prepare for eternal life.

Does God want you to be happy? Yes. But his goal isn't to make you as happy as possible at this very instant; his goal is your absolute, eternal joy in a life of perfect happiness in heaven. As a result, God often calls you to difficult acts of self-sacrifice.

> *"God, infinitely perfect and blessed in himself, in a plan of sheer goodness freely created man to make him share in his own blessed life. For this reason, at every time and in every place, God draws close to man. ... In his Son and through him, he invites men to become, in the Holy Spirit, his adopted children and thus heirs of his blessed life."*
>
> — CCC 1

MTD and the Theology of Suffering

One of the areas in which MTD is starkly different from the Catholic Faith is in its view of suffering. Catholics, of course, wish to relieve suffering whenever it is possible to do so. In the corporal works of mercy, we have a natural common ground with nonbelievers who share that goal. Catholics run into a significant barrier in connecting with nonbelievers, however, in situations in which the only way to avoid suffering is to engage in an immoral practice.

Utilitarianism is a philosophical viewpoint that seeks to maximize earthly human happiness as the highest good; MTD and utilitarianism tend to go hand in hand as the prevailing theology and philosophy of our time. As a result, practices such as euthanasia, assisted suicide, abortion, certain fertility treatments and research techniques involving human embryos, and other practices that involve the intentional mutilation or killing of innocent human beings can all be considered "good" — even necessary — to someone who seeks above all to maximize human happiness or minimize human suffering in this present life.

As evangelists, we need to be aware of the profound gulf between Christian morality and utilitarianism. To someone with a utilitarian perspective, it can seem incomprehensible — even evil — that at times the only moral choice in a difficult situation involves what seems like an option that prolongs or increases suffering. A clear understanding of Catholic moral teaching combined with sensitivity to the real desire of our friends to achieve good ends can go a long way toward gently working through these difficult issues.

Co-opting the Language of Evangelization

The second major challenge of MTD as a reigning theology is that Christian language can become confused to the point of meaninglessness. As a friend observed about the denomination he left in order to become Catholic, "We all agreed to the words of the Creed, and we all used them to mean whatever we each liked." Is God a person or just a cosmic force? Is the Incarnation the historical fact of the second person of the Holy Trinity becoming man and living on earth, fully human and fully divine, or is it a way of saying that a "Christ-like presence" was found in our midst? Is the Resurrection a historical and physical reality, or, at the death of Jesus Christ, did the Lord's presence merely continue in the loving memory and actions of his followers?

This is an area where listening and asking nonjudgmental questions can help us understand what our friend or family member believes and what barriers to faith may yet exist. We need to be aware that active, committed Catholics, including clergy and parish leaders, may be using words related to Jesus, faith, evangelization, and discipleship to mean something different from what the Church teaches. As we listen and discern, the law of charity must prevail.

Is MTD a Chasm or a Bridge?

It is easy to take a combative attitude toward MTD: "We need to correct those heathen slobs with their lazy, self-centered thinking! We need to purge the Church of its feel-good heresies!"

Yes, an intimate relationship with Jesus Christ in the Catholic Faith must be founded on the truth, the whole truth, and nothing but the truth. But when we are listening to others in the work of evangelization, whether in an intentional threshold conversation or in picking up clues by paying attention in ordinary interactions, the goal is not to charge in and play God.

Our goal is to love the other by being attentive. If, through our listening, we hear that someone is still struggling at the basic threshold of *trust*, then we know there's a need for us to offer genuine friendship. If someone is *seeking*, then we want to look for ways to water that thirst for a relationship with Jesus Christ.

In the same way, an awareness of MTD gives us a building block of common ground. Someone who affirms MTD shares a mutual belief in God, a recognition of the reality of good and evil, and an awareness that life after death, in some form, is real.

By knowing the differences between our Catholic Faith and various modern theological trends, we can be attuned to moments when someone might use "Jesus language" or "Catholic language" to describe what is really a form of deism. Regardless of how it is expressed, we can build on that common ground.

Likewise, our awareness of the overlap between MTD and Christianity can make us aware of how persons from other religious backgrounds may hold complex or nuanced beliefs quite different from what we might imagine based on our knowledge of the formal tenets of the religion they identify with. We can use our listening skills to learn more about the personal beliefs, experiences, and relationship with God of the person in front of us — not some generic Muslim or Hindu but this exact person, unique and unrepeatable. With our understanding of our friend's present faith, based in reality rather than on our preconceived ideas of what that faith should be, we now have a starting point from which we can begin to walk together toward a real relationship with Jesus Christ as revealed in the Good News.

For Reflection

- Was it difficult for you to get your mind around the difference between MTD and the Catholic Faith? What are some differences you could explain right now? What are some questions you still have?
- What questions do you have about Catholic moral teaching? What steps can you take to clear up your understanding of difficult or controversial issues?
- What are some ways you can provide consolation and support to someone facing a crisis pregnancy, infertility, or protracted, severe physical suffering?
- How has your own understanding of the Catholic Faith changed over time? What experiences helped you understand the Faith more clearly?

―――――――――――――

Saints for Evangelists

Saints Margaret Clitherow (August 30), Nicholas Owen (March 22)
The meanings of religious words are important, and *Saints Margaret Clitherow (1556–1586) and Nicholas Owen, S.J. (1562–1606),* are two of the Forty Martyrs of England and Wales whose lives and deaths attest to their belief in the meaning of the Catholic Faith. In the decades after Henry VIII declared the Church of England independent of the authority of the Catholic Church, his children's claims to the throne depended on whether their parents' marriages were valid — a matter of church law, but of what church? Thus, Catholicism was at times ruthlessly oppressed.

In an era when it was far easier to go along and simply say the words and attend the services of state-approved, almost-like-Catholic religious services, recusants were those Catholics who refused to deny the reality of the Catholic Faith. Margaret was a wife and mother who harbored and hid the outlawed priests who sneaked into the country to serve the Catholics worshiping in secret; Nicholas, a lay Jesuit brother, was a carpenter who built cleverly disguised hiding places where Catholic priests could be concealed during the search of a home. They and many other Catholics were arrested, tortured, and put to death for their faithful witness to the truth. The feast day of the Forty Martyrs of England and Wales is celebrated on May 4 in England, and October 25 in Wales.

9

The Corporal Works of Mercy

Feeding the hungry, sheltering the homeless ... we Catholics truly excel at carrying out the corporal works of mercy. Let's look at some examples of typical Catholic ministries and see how they fit with the work of evangelization. We'll see how to avoid proselytizing and what kinds of evangelization work well with a typical Catholic outreach ministry.

Key Points

- Relieving human suffering is part of our natural human vocation, but the works of mercy also have supernatural importance.
- Proselytizing is the opposite of genuine love; it is not evangelization.
- While trust-building is important, trust-building alone is not full-fledged evangelization.
- One-on-one encounters allow us to evangelize at the most personal level.

In the midst of the U.S. Civil War, a wounded soldier lay dying on the floor of a Catholic church. How had he gotten there? The triumph of Catholic nursing sisters over the virulent anti-Catholic prejudice of the mid-1800s is one of the least-told stories in American history. For thousands upon thousands of newly baptized Catholics of the 1860s, the story was a classic case of the power of evangelization through the corporal works of mercy.

The United States began as British colonies, and though freedom of religion was written into the founding documents of the Constitution, the heritage of anti-Catholic bias, descending from the legacy of the Church of England's separation from the Catholic Church, was part of the social fabric of the dominant culture.

As Irish immigration picked up during the 1840s and the 1850s, latent anti-Catholic feeling grew more intense. It was not unknown for religious superiors to instruct the sisters of their orders not to wear their habits, as it was impossible to carry out the community's work in clothing that drew unwanted attention. For many newly planted American Catholic religious communities, that work included nursing the sick.

Thus, when the Civil War broke out, Catholic nursing sisters answered the call to care for the wounded on both sides of the national divide. They proved themselves disciplined, devoted, and effective. In an era when knowledge of infection control was still sorely lacking, the cleanliness and tidiness that typified the work of the nursing sisters saved many lives. All those around them — wounded soldiers, surgeons, and the non-Catholic health-care workers charged with supervising the military's nursing system — acknowledged that the Catholic nursing sisters were far and away the most professional, dedicated, and effective nursing corps on the battlefield.

The sisters were also unabashed in their sharing of the Catholic Faith. Countless stories are told of soldiers who openly admitted that they had been taught since childhood to despise

Catholics, but who now saw, through the work of the sisters who cared for them, that what they had been raised believing was entirely wrong. In the long hours spent giving one-on-one care to the wounded soldiers, the sisters began conversations about spiritual things. In their diaries, Catholic nursing sisters describe the many conversions and baptisms that took place as they nursed the wounded.

Thanks to the work of the sisters, many soldiers recovered and went home. Others, however, were too grievously wounded to survive. The sisters urged the dying to turn to God in their last days. And thus, the dying soldier lying on the floor of a Catholic church: The young man had asked for baptism, and the sisters had carried him into the church, and he was baptized. And then, it being impossible to move him without increasing his suffering, the young man died there on the floor of the church, reconciled with God and accompanied by the nursing sisters who had loved him, body and soul.

What Are the Corporal Works of Mercy?

The corporal works of mercy are the things we do to relieve bodily suffering. We give food, drink, clothing, and shelter to those who would otherwise go without; we care for the sick and the imprisoned; we attend to the needs of the dying, the dead, and the bereaved.

These works of mercy have been the identifying feature of Christians since the very founding of the Church. Amid all the problems in the Catholic Church today, the many Catholic programs that carry out the works of mercy remain an undeniable and undimmable bright light pointing toward Our Lord.

Resisting Universalism and Pelagianism

Ironically, then, one of the challenges for those with a charism for the corporal works of mercy is overcoming the tendency *not* to evangelize. This can happen for several reasons; we'll deal here with the first two: the problems of *universalism* and *pelagianism*. They arise from an experience I've had, and I bet you have too. When it comes to the works of mercy, I have a handful of non-Christian friends who run circles around any Christian I know.

There's a reason for this. Humans are made in the image of God, and self-sacrificial love is what God is. To be fully human is to be someone who pours out his or her life for others.

I look with admiration at the fearless generosity of my atheist, agnostic, and pagan friends and can only strive to follow their example. How then, we wonder, could someone who is so kind and generous possibly be headed to hell? Most Catholics find themselves falling into two lines of faulty thinking:

Universalism is the belief that no one goes to hell, except maybe Hitler. After all, most people have good hearts, even if they aren't perfect, right?

Pelagianism is the belief that we are saved by our good works. Our non-Christian friends do good things, and that should count for something, shouldn't it?

Both of these ideas — the theology of the pretty-good person — are built on kernels of truth. When I look at someone through God's eyes, I am looking through the eyes of love. I am seeing the inherent goodness and worth of God's creation. God wills that this person be saved. When I see my non-Christian friend acting with self-sacrifice, I am seeing my friend live out his or her God-given mission to love others as God loves.

But here's the simple fact: If I decide that this is good enough, I am ignoring the reality that Our Lord warned against the dangers of hell and emphatically stated that salvation comes through him alone. I am ignoring God's plan for how he wishes to save us.

In the Acts of the Apostles, after the descent of the Holy Spirit, Saint Peter is empowered to preach to the people who have gathered from all over the world about the reality of Christ's sacrifice for us. When he is done proclaiming the Good News, we learn the means by which God extends salvation: "Now when they heard this they were cut to the heart, and said to Peter and the rest of the apostles, 'Brethren, what shall we do?' And Peter said to them, 'Repent and be baptized every one of you in the name of Jesus Christ for the forgiveness of your sins; and you shall receive the gift of the Holy Spirit' " (Acts 2:37–38).

Yes, we trust the souls of the deceased to Our Lord's all-loving mercy. But we have been specifically told to go and make disciples. We have been commanded to lead all to belief in Jesus Christ in the Catholic Faith. When we ignore the Lord's command to us, we aren't just depriving our friends and loved ones of the path of salvation that God wishes to give them; we are also courting a significant risk to our own souls in presuming to know better than God what our friends need.

> **"The Church's deepest nature is expressed in her three-fold responsibility: of proclaiming the word of God (kerygma-martyria), celebrating the sacraments (leitourgia), and exercising the ministry of charity (diakonia). These duties presuppose each other and are inseparable.**
> **For the Church, charity is not a kind of welfare activity which could equally well be left to others, but is a part of her nature, an indispensable expression of her very being."**
> — Pope Benedict XVI, *Deus Caritas Est*, "On Christian Love," 2005

The Catholic Faith Is Not for Rent

Another reason Catholics may be hesitant to evangelize through the works of mercy is due to a healthy fear of proselytizing. As we discussed in the opening chapter, *proselytizing* is the act of taking advantage of someone's vulnerability to strong-arm that person into an outward practice of the Faith. If you have spent much time around addicts seeking financial support, you know how the game works: The addict recites the required lines about regret and a desire to change, in exchange for the benefactor's handing over of material goods.

One of the beauties of the Catholic programs I have worked with over the years is that there is a scrupulous avoidance of any hint of proselytizing. If you show up at Catholic Charities needing clothing and a shower, you are given clothing and a shower. No one asks you to sit through a video about Jesus or raise your hand to commit yourself to Christ — you don't have to pay for the help you receive by making an outward show of faith.

I see the same thing at St. Vincent de Paul Society meals. Yes, there is a giant crucifix in the dining room; yes, there is grace before the meal. But the meal is given freely and generously, yours because you showed up, no questions asked. I could list countless other Catholic missions that embody this same ethic of giving freely, with no regard for the religion, or lack of religion, of the recipients. In this way, we stay firmly in the territory of true evangelization. Let's see how that can happen.

The Works of Mercy Build Trust

In our five stages of evangelization and discipleship, the first was *trust*. When people experience kindness at the hands of Catholics, whether during treatment at a Catholic hospital, in a program for the homeless, or in the generosity of a Catholic friend who sees a neighbor's need and makes an effort to help, this kindness overcomes suspicion, fear, and past hurts. The mathematics of kindness are simple: Healing actions are healing.

When we serve others selflessly, we demonstrate to ourselves and to the world that we truly believe the Catholic Faith. If our lives are just as self-absorbed as everyone else's, revolving around our own comfort and security, then it becomes evident to outsiders that our faith is just a decoration. When we act on our faith, then people stand up and take notice.

Getting Beyond Trust

Building trust, however, is just the first step on the path toward a relationship with Jesus Christ. In order for our works of mercy to be fully evangelizing, we have to learn from those Civil War nursing sisters. We must build one-on-one relationships, and we must be comfortable in talking about our own relationships with God.

Building one-on-one relationships means that assembly-line programs are not sufficient. That doesn't mean we can't have situations where a corps of volunteers shows up and does chores. Pure manpower is needed to perform the works of mercy. But the real evangelization is done by the person who commits to living in genuine community with an individual who needs love and companionship.

Living in community means you speak to each other regularly. It means you take time to listen and find out what it going on in the other's life. It means you spend time together. It means you make sacrifices to care for the other.

One-on-one attention is consuming. I can scoop mashed potatoes or hand out bags of clothing for dozens of people a day. I can truly befriend only a few.

For those Civil War nurses, this befriending took place in the context of endless hours of carrying out menial, revolting chores, tending to the hundreds and thousands of wounded in the bloodiest conflict the nation had ever known. (As a friend of mine who is an ICU nurse puts it: "I had no idea my job would be mostly about managing poop." Talent for nursing is a gift.) In the course of a long, busy day, the reality is that a nursing sister cannot develop a deep spiritual relationship with every patient in her care.

But she can be open to opportunities to build such relationships when the chance arises.

Likewise, there's a balance to be found in all our other works of mercy. Those who bring clean-water services to developing nations work on two levels: water for the multitudes, and spiritual friendship for the handful whom God happens to place in just the right circumstances to allow a deeper relationship to grow. Those who provide showers and clean clothes to the homeless outfit dozens upon dozens of recipients a week; but the evangelizer also has eyes and heart open to one-on-one friendships.

In a Catholic program of mercy, the pyramid of evangelization might look like this:

The Base of Busyness

At the foundation level of our program, we provide a basic service to many people, carried out in a kind, courteous manner. We can build trust at this level, but we are too busy serving too many people to be able to make personal connections. Still, it is possible for miracles to happen. Certain gifted saints were able to bring thousands and thousands to conversion because they had a charism for speaking just the right words to turn the hearts of many listeners at once. We don't all have that gift.

The Middle Moments

Through prayerful attentiveness and cheerful conversation, we provide encouragement and momentary companionship to many whom we get to know only briefly. At this level, if we are attuned to the Holy Spirit's leading, we can step in and offer a small amount of help at any point on the path of the five thresholds of conversion. It is possible that a few exchanged words or a single gesture of kindness will be a life-changing moment for someone we meet — and we might never even know how much impact we had.

The Personal Point

The top of a pyramid has very little room in it, but it "gets to the point." With just one or a very few persons, we can develop a deep, lasting friendship that allows us to provide continuous, ongoing companionship on the path toward closer union with Jesus Christ. This is evangelization at its fullest and deepest. Many people will never develop a relationship with Jesus Christ unless somebody somewhere befriends them at this level.

All three levels of the pyramid are important. God weaves together relationships at all three levels, allowing many evangelists to each play their part in the conversion of a soul.

Evangelization Happens One Soul at a Time

We don't need formal programs to carry out works of mercy. In our families, neighborhoods, and workplaces, there are people who need our care and support. When we choose to build an ongoing relationship of mutual help with someone we know, we are operating at the personal point of evangelization. The tip-top of the pyramid, where it seems as if the fewest people are being served, is the place where the most work is being accomplished.

Think about it. In a large-scale service program, it's simply impossible for me to get to know the deep needs and worries of every person I meet. In contrast, if I regularly spend long hours getting to know someone and doing what I can to help that person, I have so much ability to listen and learn. Over time, we can open up to each other and truly get to know each other. Over time, we can move past the superficial conversations and accompany each other on a closer walk toward the Lord.

This is evangelization. What does this mean for the works of mercy? It means that the best programs are only effective past the trust level, when we find ways of building deep, lasting, individual, one-soul-at-a-time friendships with those who check in at our hospital for sinners.

For Reflection

- Does your social life tend to lean toward many casual friendships or a few deep relationships?
- Which of the corporal works of mercy have you carried out?
- Are there any works of mercy that particularly interest you?
- If you volunteer with a service program, what are some ways you can use that platform to build a close friendship with one or a few people among the many you serve?
- Is there someone in your private life you are serving now? Is there someone you might be able to serve?
- How can you grow more attuned to opportunities for one-on-one service that God puts in your life?

Saints for Evangelists

Saint Mary Catherine of Saint Augustine (May 8)

Saint Mary Catherine of Saint Augustine (1632–1668) was born in France, and from an early age, she showed concern for the sick and the poor. She entered into religious life in 1644 and, at the age of sixteen, volunteered to sail for Quebec, where the sisters were asked to run a hospital for the poor and the needy.

When she arrived at the hospital, she immediately set to work taking care of both the physical and spiritual needs of the patients. She learned the languages of the indigenous peoples so that she could better serve them and committed herself to prayer and penance in support of her missionary work.

She was given responsibility both for managing the finances of the hospital and training new members of the community; despite her intense workload, she was known throughout the community for her kind, tender disposition toward others. Because of her self-sacrifice for both the European colonists and the native inhabitants of the region, she is considered one of the six founders of the Catholic Church in Canada.

10

The Power of Beauty

Believe it or not, there is something called evangelization through beauty, and it works. What is it? How do we stir up the innate human longing for all that is true, beautiful, and good? In this chapter, we will begin by focusing primarily on the concept of beauty and then see how to apply this mode of evangelization in a similar way to any other human pursuit.

Key Points

- Every human soul longs for the perfect truth, beauty, and goodness of heaven.
- Jesus Christ is Truth, Beauty, and Goodness.
- For us, as persons created in the image of God, this path of evangelization is part of our original mission.
- Everything true, beautiful, and good brings glory to God and draws others closer to him.

On a Sunday afternoon in August, my children and I strolled through the cathedral in Strasbourg, France. Amid soaring arches and intricate stained glass, the organ came to life. The cathedral choir, assembled on risers in the middle of the nave, serenaded us wandering tourists with enchanting classical hymnody. We spent an hour surrounded by some of the most beautiful art in the entire world, created by the faithful over centuries.

As we explored the aisles and the altars of the cathedral, we came upon stations where visitors were encouraged to stop and light candles. Gentle, seeker-friendly signs invited those who might not even know how to pray to take a moment in the quiet shadows of the cathedral to reach out to God with a thought, a few words, or just an inner longing.

This is evangelization by beauty.

We Are Made for Heaven

What is it that drives us to spruce up the house and the yard, spend hours shopping for that perfect outfit, or sigh with admiration at a glamorous movie star? It isn't that we're hopelessly shallow. It's that deep within ourselves is a longing for the One who is Perfect Beauty itself.

So, yes, all our chasing after heaven-on-earth is vain and shallow. We won't find satisfaction here. But also, it isn't vain and shallow. Because we are persons made in the image of God, creating beautiful things is one of our jobs. It's part of our mission.

Beauty Is More Than Prettiness

In an effort to answer that call as co-creators of beauty, we sometimes settle for mere prettiness. Pretty things invoke the beautiful: the swish of a skirt, a neatly laid table, a fresh haircut. These are all good.

Beauty, though, is deeper than mere prettiness. Pretty is the baby's heirloom christening gown; beauty is the painful, messy, exhausting work of pregnancy and childbirth. Pretty is the family all dressed up for Christmas; beauty is bringing Christmas to that stinking man who sleeps on the bench in the park. Pretty is the parish church freshly cleaned top to bottom and filled with flowers for Easter; beauty is the work-worn bodies that did the cleaning.

All these pretty things are beautiful inasmuch as they reflect a greater beauty: the christening gown that represents generations of sacrificial love; the family whose domestic church revolves around serving Jesus Christ in all his guises; the parish whose members want to honor the Lord in all they do, at Mass and in the world.

A Tale of Two Churches

Let me tell you a story about how a surprise encounter with the Lord worked in my life.

Long ago, before I had children and before I returned to the Catholic Church, my husband had a business trip to Hawaii. One day while he was in meetings, I took the rental car and went for a drive. At a small town, I stopped for lunch. On the town square, as in many small towns across America, were several local churches. Two churches had their doors open for visitors.

The first church I visited was a lovely historic Episcopalian building. On a shelf in the rear were evangelizing brochures; I took one that ended up being very inspiring and helpful for me. I admired the old stonework and was truly grateful that the pastor had chosen to open the door to strangers like me, offering a cool, quiet place to rest and pray.

The second church was Catholic. It was not a historic building. It was one of those bland 1970s buildings, complete with tacky brown carpet and inarticulate squiggles trying to pass for abstract art. There were no helpful brochures on a shelf in the back.

Also, it was breathtaking.

Even as someone who had not yet returned to the fullness of the Faith, I could feel the Real Presence of Jesus Christ in the Holy Eucharist from the moment I walked in the door. I was moved to prayer in a way I hadn't been in ages.

The Episcopalians had a much prettier building. The Catholics had Beauty himself.

The Both-And Custodians of True Beauty

Do you remember what Adam and Eve used to do for a living, back before Original Sin? They were the keepers of a garden. They were appointed custodians of God's breathtakingly beautiful creation, commanded to make it more beautiful by filling it with countless little images of God, each one called to care for the earthly paradise and cultivate its beauty.

That was our original mission, and before the Fall, that mission was literally a walk in the park.

Now we struggle. Now we toil to scratch out a living; now we co-create beauty only with drudgery and pain. Our Lord is in it with us, offering the greatest sacrifice, the greatest toil, the greatest pain, with which to redeem all our works and save us from our sins.

But our mission is not lost; it is only transformed. Our work on earth is, as it always has been, a preparation for the fullness of eternal life in perfect union with God.

As Catholics, we don't have to choose between prettiness and true beauty. We can have the Real Presence and well-designed churches. We can have a truly welcoming parish and gorgeous vestments. We can have the cathedral with its doors open to all comers, and the symphony of sacred art within.

When we evangelize through beauty, we do so in two steps. First, we put our hearts in order. We put God first in our every thought and action, so that all we do may be "motivated by a pure love of him," to paraphrase a time-honored prayer. Then, fueled by that love, we seek the good of others. We seek to guide others toward Jesus Christ using every tool at our disposal, including creating beautiful, tranquil, welcoming refuges from our sin-darkened world.

> *"This world in which we live needs beauty in order not to sink into despair. It is beauty, like truth, which brings joy to the heart of man and is that precious fruit which resists the wear and tear of time, which unites generations and makes them share things in admiration. And all of this is through your hands. May these hands be pure and disinterested. Remember that you are the guardians of beauty in the world. May that suffice to free you from tastes which are passing and have no genuine value, to free you from the search after strange or unbecoming expressions. Be always and everywhere worthy of your ideals and you will be worthy of the Church which, by our voice, addresses to you today her message of friendship, salvation, grace and benediction."*
>
> — Pope Paul VI, Address to Artists, December 8, 1965

The World Is Ugly

This type of evangelization is meant to be poured out generously. When my children and I stepped into that cathedral in Strasbourg, no one asked if we were Catholic. No one asked if we were good enough, or appreciative enough, or wise enough to be worthy of the breathtaking beauty within. It was simply there, open to us and anyone else who wanted to come and see.

When we evangelize through truth, beauty, and goodness,

we who are the Body of Christ use the Little Way of Saint Thérèse, "doing small things with great love" to create a refuge for those who are beaten down by the ugliness of our fallen world. We reach souls who are seeking something that lasts, something more than the superficiality of our culture.

Preeminent in this path of evangelization is communicating the Lord's presence in the arts. In beautiful gardens and natural areas, music, architecture, painting, and sculpture, we make truth, beauty, and goodness something we can see, hear, touch, and smell. Many people who struggle with prayer find that the arts provide the way of praying that draws them closest to God.

Sometimes we will use our words to share the message of beauty and goodness. One of the pitfalls of parish life is that we often try to disciple those who still need to be evangelized. I might, for example, want to thrust a talk on chastity at a group of teens preparing for confirmation, because I know that part of being a Christian disciple is learning to live chastely. But, as we know, not everyone seeking the sacraments has reached the threshold of discipleship — even those who come to Mass of their own choice and are excited about doing Catholic stuff might still be only at the stage of *trust* or *curiosity*. So if I speak of chastity in terms of "this is what you as a Christian believer need to do," then my words are likely to fall flat.

But all of us, no matter what threshold we stand on, long to be loved. No matter how far from God someone is, I know that if I speak not of rules and regulations but of a call to love and be loved, my words are likely to resonate. I probably won't persuade my listener to start living chastely immediately (though I might), but I can extend a glimmer of hope: No, relationships shouldn't be empty and meaningless. No, you don't deserve to be treated like a piece of meat. Yes, there is something out there, another way, that is so much more beautiful. Let me tell you about real romance. Let me tell you a story of love and sacrifice and heroism and intimacy.

Truth, beauty, and goodness can be communicated in our actions, as in the works of mercy. In the sciences, we discover the truth about the God's creation — think of how many pro-life arguments are simply the stating of scientific facts. Likewise, there's truth, beauty, and goodness in a well-formed spreadsheet or an accurate set of financial documents. We can, through good business practices, reject the idea of "every man for himself" and provide a beacon of honesty, integrity, and generosity for those who have given up on the idea that truth and goodness even exist.

> *"Finally, the arts modeled on the supreme exemplar of all beauty which is God Himself, from whom is derived all the beauty to be found in nature, are more securely withdrawn from vulgar concepts and more efficaciously rise towards the ideal, which is the life of all art"*
> — Pope Pius X, *Iucunda Sane*, "On Pope Gregory the Great," 1904

Evangelizing Through the True, the Beautiful, and the Good

At the Catholic Writers Guild, my fellow authors frequently discuss what makes literature Catholic. The answer is not that the story contains Catholic characters (though it might) or explicitly Catholic themes (though it might), but that it meets the threefold test of true, beautiful, and good. In the truth department, a work of fiction is *true* when it accurately reflects the deeper reality of creation and of the human heart, even if the story is told using fantastical elements. A story is beautiful when it is well-crafted. A story is good when it inspires the reader to greater virtue and holiness. This inspiration to virtue doesn't have to come — indeed, generally should not come — through a heavy-handed morality tale. Rather, the reader is inspired by seeing a character overcome danger and self-deception in order to do what is right, even at great personal cost. Thus, a romance, a mystery, or a thriller can be inspiring Catholic literature without ever saying a word about anything Catholic whatsoever.

The same is true in all the arts. A painting or a piece of music can be explicitly religious, but it can also attest to the true, the beautiful, and the good in this world through purely secular or even entirely abstract themes.

And yet we often fight against our callings as artists. Your craft may seem too humble to make a difference, or your talent too limited. If you are an artist of any kind, you may experience the struggle of wondering whether the time and aggravation of your almost pathologically inescapable calling is even worth it. What good are you doing in the world? The whole thing probably isn't even making you any money. And yet what does it profit God to create haunting windswept landscapes, achingly distant stars, or the daily dramatic overtures of sunrise and sunset? When you practice your humble art, you are living out your vocation as a person made in the image of God, and your obedience to that calling allows others to know God through you.

But suppose your art seems purely mercenary. Are you a lawyer? An accountant? An engineer? Perhaps you slog away at a dead-end job strictly for the purpose of putting food on the table. All human work has the capacity to convey the true, the beautiful, and the good. If authors and film directors must fight the urge to produce lurid pulp in order to rake in the profits, in the practical arts all workers must fight the pressure to carry out immoral practices in order to get ahead — or even just to stay afloat. In fighting this fight, we grow in virtue and become those beacons, those lamps, shining for those around us who are struggling with temptation and perhaps don't know how to escape the traps in which they find themselves.

More than this, the workaday world abounds with opportunities to create the true, the beautiful, and the good. Think about how different it feels to receive an ugly or confusing email as opposed to receiving a clear, carefully worded one. Think about what it's like to stop at the store and be able to find what you need easily and efficiently. Think about what it's like to stop to use the bathroom and find the place clean and pleasant! Think about what it's like to have an honest lawyer defending your case, or a good engineer designing your highway, or a good accountant ensuring that your financial statements are in order. Your life is different when professionals at every level do their work, however mundane or humble, with integrity.

The effects of evangelization through truth, beauty, and goodness, are not always visible. This is a mode through which the Holy Spirit may open a private conversation with the beloved. Inspiration or delight may provoke an internal process of questioning or striving that no other person ever sees. Other times, the response to truth, beauty, and goodness may lead to overt questions about our lives as Christians, our goals and purposes, or how we find the strength to live differently.

Thus, none of us ought to neglect our small part in this way of bringing the presence of God to others. Evangelization through the true, the beautiful, and the good is carried out in a very targeted manner at Catholic institutions and, in fact, is a calling for every Catholic, no matter what our state in life might be.

For Reflection

- What kinds of beauty do you find particularly moving? Music? Some kind of art or craft? The natural world?
- When has something true, beautiful, or good drawn you closer to God?
- Have you ever felt that your daily work was pointless,

only to have someone finally show gratitude for your labor? How did that change your understanding of your vocation?

- How does your personal mission or state in life, whatever it might be, help bring truth, beauty, and goodness to others?

Saints for Evangelists

Saint Lazarus Zographos (February 23)

Saint Lazarus Zographos (810–867) was a monk in Constantinople known for his love of Christ, his prayer, his self-control, his almsgiving ... and his artwork. Unfortunately, he lived during a period of the iconoclastic controversy. When Emperor Theophilos came to power, he banned the creation of sacred images and ordered existing images to be destroyed.

Saint Lazarus ignored the ban and continued to make beautiful sacred art and worked as well to restore artwork that was damaged by iconoclasts (the people who thought it was wrong to paint images of holy things). The emperor threatened him with death, but since Saint Lazarus was a priest, that wasn't legal. Instead, he was put in prison and tortured to the point that it seemed surely he would die. As he lay on his deathbed, the empress pleaded for Lazarus to be released from prison.

Miraculously, Saint Lazarus recovered from his wounds and went on to resume painting and restoring sacred art. Some of his post-torture icons are credited with the power to perform cures and miracles.

11

The Liturgy Link

How does the Mass fit into our efforts at evangelization? The answer is complicated, but there are ways you can help people discover God in the Mass, whether you are a pastor, an active parishioner, or a visitor bringing a friend to sit with you in the pews.

Key Points

- The Mass is not by its nature an evangelizing event.
- "Get them to Mass!" cannot be the limit of our evangelizing work.
- Regardless of our liturgical tradition, the Mass should be centered on the reverent, solemn, and joyful worship of God.
- When we invite a non-Catholic or lapsed Catholic to Mass, we should plan ahead to make sure our friend has the information and companionship necessary to understand what is happening.
- The Mass is the center of the evangelizer's life.

There are good reasons why we instinctively think "invite them to Mass" when we think of evangelization. We know that human happiness is ultimately found only in a relationship with God and that we are made for heaven — and heaven is made present for us every day in the Mass.

We also sometimes confuse cause and effect. We know that disciples go to Mass, and that if someone is not attending Mass (barring illness or other exemptions), he or she is not a disciple. Therefore, our brains tell us that if our friends start coming to Mass, then everything will be all better.

And of course, we just want to share our joy. We love Jesus, and so we love his Mass. Any decent human being would want others to revel in the peace and strength that come from the highest form of worship available this side of eternity.

All that is well and good. The trouble is that the Mass is not meant to evangelize.

Not a Tent Revival

The Mass is a meeting of Creator and creature, in a manner that assumes we have, through baptism and personal conversion, received the grace of a restored relationship with God. The Mass assumes that we are able to truly *assist*, as the expression has it — that, in keeping with our age and ability, we are able to join our prayers with those of the priest and congregation, in doing the spiritual work that happens in the Mass.

Now, because God is indeed the Hound of Heaven, and it is not we but the Holy Spirit who works in souls to bring about conversion, there is no reason the Lord cannot speak heart to heart with whomever he calls. Someone can wander in off the street and fall in love with Jesus and the Catholic Faith almost by accident, it seems at times, for God is able to work such conversions.

But many times God will work through ordinary humans like us, through a long, slow process of listening, building relationships, and slowly growing closer to Christ over time. In such cases, someone might not be ready — spiritually, intellectually, or even physically — to assist at Mass in a way that helps him or her grow closer to Christ. Therefore, we should not assume that an evangelization strategy of "get them to Mass, and our work is done" is always fruitful or is even a good idea.

Ready or Not, Here They Come

Even though the Mass isn't meant to be our primary vehicle of evangelization, we still must, to some extent, acknowledge that it often is.

The homilist has the thankless job of preaching both to the converted and to those in the pews who are resistant to the Faith. Those who don't believe may, sadly, include many parish leaders. There will be no pleasing everyone, but a faithful, charitable, and factually accurate homily can go a long way with any audience.

Beyond that, let the Mass be the Mass: our ultimate act of worship, making present the sacrifice of Jesus Christ.

What Should the Liturgy Be Like?

The Church is both the guardian of the ancient and unchanging mystery of the divine liturgy, and a fruitful mother whose children across time and place have embodied that liturgy in a variety of rites that take into account the local language and customs. In a pluralistic culture, we can anticipate that all legitimate options will have their place.

In regard to the Liturgy Wars, then, the question is not "Is there something inherently wrong with this form of the Mass that the Church in her wisdom has handed down to us?" The question, rather, is "Given that this or that approved form of the divine liturgy is an option for us, when and how shall we choose to render it, so that souls can find intimacy and wonder in the Presence of Jesus Christ?"

In chapter 16, "Crafting Parish Events," we will explore some options for prayer and devotions outside of Mass that can be helpful in taking pressure off the pastor and the music director where the Mass is concerned.

What Not to Do at Mass

Though I can complain about church music with the best of them, I recognize that even options for the Mass that are not to my taste may be helpful for souls different from mine. There have been times when I was traveling and found myself visiting a parish where just the sort of sermon or ambiance or hymn that I usually love to hate happened to be exactly what my soul needed that morning, and I am moved to tears by God's ability to work through the humblest of mechanisms.

As a result, I leave arguing about the liturgy to other forums. Still, we can say with certainty that select disastrous effects must be avoided.

I have visited parishes where the sound was so blaringly painful that one of my young children hid under the pew with ears covered — and I felt that my child had made a reasonable decision. I have watched a priest stand before the congregation and accuse a group of children, including a little girl of eight years old who had made her first holy Communion only weeks before, of being "holier than the Church" because they followed a liturgical custom practiced at other parishes in the same diocese, with the approval of their bishop. I have been appalled to discover that a parish had summarily locked the doors to all wheelchair-accessible entrances as a security measure, making no provision for the disabled to enter the building other than to wait outside on the sidewalk and flag down a passerby for assistance.

These and other shocking practices were carried about by otherwise decent Christians. If I were to name the priests responsible for these offenses, I would be naming sincere, loving men who sacrifice constantly in order to make Christ present to others. The lesson is not that a seemingly good priest is really a rotter; the lesson is that any of us can unwittingly commit some thoughtless action that scorches souls with what ought to be the universal beacon of hope.

The Mass for Evangelization

Despite the fact that the Mass is not, by its nature, an evangelizing event, at every stage of evangelization there are reasons it might be prudent to invite a friend to Mass.

To shed light on the mystery of what happens at Mass. A non-Catholic friend in good faith once asked me what happens at Mass. "So you go into that closet and confess your sins to a priest?" was the question. Um, no, I explained, that's not Mass. My friend's knowledge of the Catholic Faith consisted of scenes in movies and television shows, where visits to the confessional far outweigh scenes of people attending Mass.

To satisfy curiosity. Another friend asked to come to Mass with me; as a pastor's wife, for many years she had been unable to attend services at any congregation but her own. Now that her husband had retired from ministry, she was enjoying going around to see how "church" was done in other denominations.

To put to rest misconceptions, to answer questions about Catholic practices, or introduce the possibility of participating in Catholic worship.

To answer spiritual longing. When someone is seeking God, Mass is the obvious place to find him. As we accompany a friend who is on the path toward Jesus, it is reasonable to suggest: "Why don't you come worship with me on Sunday? You don't have to decide to be Catholic. Just enjoy being there and enjoy the time spent with God, participating only as far as you feel comfortable." Assisting at Mass, under the right circumstances, can be ideal for someone grappling with his or her relationship with God, because the Mass is such a naturally reflective and meditative experience.

As preparation for entering the Church. It sometimes happens that someone is on the cusp of converting and has never attended Mass. In that case, it's high time the invitation was extended.

> *"'The sacred liturgy does not exhaust the entire activity of the Church': it must be preceded by evangelization, faith, and conversion. It can then produce its fruits in the lives of the faithful: new life in the Spirit, involvement in the mission of the Church, and service to her unity."*
> — CCC 1072

Tips for Bringing a Friend to Mass
Prepare ahead for the Communion question.
Explain that receiving holy Communion is a public proclamation to God and man that you fully believe, accept, and profess all that the Catholic Church teaches. If your friend is, in fact, ready to join the Church, get him or her to RCIA on the double.

Anticipate difficulties.
Provide a short overview of what happens at Mass, and give a heads-up on anything that might be confusing or worrisome. This could be something as practical as explaining to your friend with the knee injury that he or she is not obliged to kneel with the congregation. Before bringing some non-Catholic colleagues one day to daily Mass, held in a teeny-tiny chapel where every voice would be clearly heard, a friend and I gave the warning that there would be a pause in the Lord's Prayer after "deliver us from evil."

You won't do this perfectly. Another time, a difficulty I didn't anticipate was telling my good friends attending my son's baptism that the sign of peace is not the end of Mass. Everyone shook hands and greeted each other, and my friends figured it must be the end of the service, because that's what happened at the end of their church service. It didn't help that in our tiny parish, it was not uncommon for friends to walk up and down the aisle, greeting one another, during a very extended exchange of peace. My friends gathered coats and purses and started to go ... then realized no one else was leaving and sneaked back to their seats for the remainder of the liturgy.

Bring a good children's missal.

It is fine quietly and respectfully to provide a few brief explanations of what is happening at Mass as the liturgy proceeds. Though canon law does not require it, your parish probably sticks to the time-honored rule that the music sung by the congregation must be spread across a minimum of three documents, so you'll want to help your friend flip from book to book. And even if your friend is a grown-up, a well-chosen children's missal is the easiest way to follow along with both the letter and spirit of what is happening at Mass. If you like, you can cover it with other paper so nobody will know that your friend is using a children's missal.

The Eucharist as the Source and Summit of Our Faith

The Mass is the beginning and the end of our spiritual lives as Catholics. It is the source, in that we are fed and formed as Christians through our time spent with Christ in the Holy Eucharist. It is our summit, in that the whole of our Christian life is oriented toward knowing, loving, and serving God; this side of heaven, that holy union with God is embodied most perfectly in a well-prayed Mass.

Above all, then, the Mass's place in evangelization is central — not because it is the "event" that we invite our non-Christian friends to attend but because from the Mass we evangelizers receive our ability and our purpose. Through the graces of the sacraments, God endows us with the gifts we need to carry out our mission; our mission is ordered in the service of those sacraments.

When we consider the liturgy from the evangelist's perspective, then, we have one purpose that is above all others: How can I learn to love God better in the Holy Mass?

If I make that one goal my chief purpose, the rest of my evangelization efforts will fall into place.

For Reflection

- What have been some of your best experiences of the Holy Mass? What gifts would you say your parish has when it comes to praying the Mass well?
- When have you been surprised by God's movement in your soul at Mass?
- To what extent is the Mass the center of your life in Jesus Christ? To what extent is it the center of the life of your ministry?
- What is your state in life (layperson, deacon, religious, priest, pastor, bishop …)? Based on your state in life and your role in your parish, your diocese, or your religious community, what are your personal responsibilities regarding worship at Mass? What responsibilities belong to someone else? How can you make your role in the Mass a more reverent time of worshiping Jesus Christ?

Saints for Evangelists

Saint Peter of Saint Joseph de Betancur (April 25)

Saint Peter of Saint Joseph de Betancur (1626–1667) was born in the Canary Islands. After a childhood of poverty and servitude, he made his way to Guatemala, where he joined family members who had settled there. In 1653, he enrolled in the seminary but gave up after three years because he was unable to keep up academically. He didn't, however, give up on his vocation of evangelization or his devotion to the Holy Mass. Instead, he rented a house near a church and began teaching the children of the poor.

Over time, others joined him in his work of serving the poor, the sick, and the imprisoned, and he had no choice but to form a religious community, which became part of the Franciscan community. (Peter was a Franciscan tertiary, a layperson who belongs to the order.) He funded Masses to be said in the early hours of the morning, a practice that subsidized the livings of poor priests while making it possible for the poor to attend Mass before they had to get to work — a practice emulated today by priests who schedule "last chance" and early-morning Masses to fit the schedules of those who work irregular hours.

12

The Role of Apologetics

"Apologetics" means explaining and defending the Catholic Faith. When and how can you use apologetics to help people grow closer to God? When should you hush your mouth and offer a big hug instead?

Key Points

- People become Catholic for many reasons. They stay Catholic because Catholicism is true.
- There are good, sound, logical answers for the questions people have about the Catholic Faith.
- We should prepare ourselves to respond accurately and charitably to objections to the Faith in a way that is most helpful to our listeners.
- Sometimes a friend's question is not a request for information but a cry for help. We must be attentive to the deeper spiritual needs that may lie behind a difficult question.

Here are some questions people have asked me about the Catholic Faith:

"Why do Catholics venerate Mary and the saints?"

"How can an all-powerful God be good if he allows such evil in the world?"

"How can we know that God even exists?"

"Where in the Bible do we find priests, the Mass, and the Eucharist?"

"Is the Bible even reliable? What about contradictions within the Bible?"

"How can you belong to the Church when there are so many scandals involving her leaders, even at the highest levels?"

"Do Catholics hate gay people?"

"Why doesn't the Catholic Church approve of birth control?"

"What makes the Catholic Church any different from the religion I grew up with? How do I know that its teachings are true?"

There's another question I get asked as well: "Why are you Catholic?"

When people ask me how I became Catholic, I tell the story I shared earlier in this book, of a spiritual journey involving a powerful moment of personal conversion. But when they ask why I am Catholic now, my answer is much shorter: I am Catholic because Catholicism is true.

End of story.

This is why we evangelize. Not because Catholicism is helpful for some people, nor because we have good programs to keep running nor because we provide a warm, friendly place to make friends and build community. We aren't Catholic for the music; we aren't Catholic for the job opportunities; we aren't Catholic for fame and fortune.

The reason we are Catholic is because Catholicism is true.

The reason we evangelize — the reason we try to help others find their way into deep, personal relationships with Jesus in the context of the Catholic Faith — is that Catholicism is true.

If it were not true, you'd be wasting your time.

But it is true, and therefore, when people have questions or worries about the Catholic Faith, there are good explanations you can share in response. The art of explaining and defending the Catholic Faith is called "apologetics," and it fills an important role in the process of evangelization and discipleship.

The Story of Three Converts

Every now and then, you meet someone who literally read his or her way into the Catholic Church. For a certain type of person, the path to Jesus involves examining and testing the claims of the Church. This sort of convert might spend hours and hours debating with a good sparring partner, loving every minute of it, and eventually recognizing that it's time to see about walking into a Catholic church for the first time. There are people who make the decision to become Catholic solely on the basis of research and logical analysis and meet Catholics or attend Mass only after they have made the personal decision to accept the Catholic Faith.

For this reason, in your outreach to friends, family members, and total strangers, it is important to be able to give good, logical, well-researched answers to questions that people have about the Catholic Faith.

Call this perfect audience for apologetics Convert Type 3. Why number three? Because this is the least-common type of person who needs apologetics.

Who's Type 2? Think back to my husband Jon's conversion story. He and I spent a lot of time arguing about the Catholic Faith, but Jon wasn't really looking to be talked into Catholicism. He did, however, need to have a lot of his fears and concerns put to rest so that he could be confident of his decision to be Catholic. When he first returned to the Church, he still wasn't completely comfortable with the entirety of the Catholic Faith. Apologetics got him far enough over the hump so that when he felt a spiritual need that only the Catholic Church could answer, he was able to put a foot in Catholic waters despite still having some doubts.

Many people won't be argued into the Church, but they do need certain worrisome questions answered before they are able to set aside concerns and focus on deeper issues.

If all Catholic converts came from outside the Church, of course we'd have only Type 3 and Type 2. But we don't. The largest audience for apologetics are the converts sitting right there in the pews at your local parish.

Remember my story? I returned to the Catholic Church through a powerful experience of personal conversion, and the people who evangelized me weren't even Catholic! They certainly weren't making logical arguments in favor of the Catholic Faith.

For me, and for most people who are Catholic, apologetics comes after the initial decision to become Catholic.

Apologetics for the already Catholic can serve many purposes:

- to help someone who is culturally Catholic to see the objective reality of the Catholic Faith, leading to a stronger, deeper conversion
- to reassure someone struggling with doubts about the Faith by laying out the evidence for the truth of what we believe
- to put into words ideas about the Faith that a cradle Catholic might have "always known" but never been able to explain clearly
- to grow stronger and more knowledgeable about the Catholic Faith as part of growing as a disciple of Jesus Christ
- to gain confidence in the ability to answer others' questions about the Catholic Faith

One apologetics skill that evangelists need in every case is the ability to proclaim the Gospel in our explanations. Chapter 24, on catechesis, includes some examples of how to do that.

> **"Apart from the supernatural help of God, nothing is better calculated to heal those minds and to bring them into favor with the Catholic faith than the solid doctrine of the Fathers and the Scholastics, who so clearly and forcibly demonstrate the firm foundations of the faith, its divine origin, its certain truth, the arguments that sustain it."**
> — Pope Leo XIII, *Aeterni Patris*, "On the Restoration of Christian Philosophy," 1879

How to Use Apologetics in Evangelization

I am a big believer in the importance of apologetics. I also know that hot-headed Catholics like myself can get into big trouble when we get carried away in the joy of a good argument. Here are a few tips for making sure that we use our superpowers for good and not evil:

Avoid arguing for the sake of arguing.

As much fun as it is to dissect every little error, don't be that person who quibbles constantly. Learn to discern when it is time to debate and when it is time to practice prayerful silence.

Listen!

Your goal as an apologist is to get to the heart of your friend's real questions, not waste time bickering over trivialities. Intense listening, combined with asking thought-provoking questions, can clear away the mental clutter and shine light on the area where your friend's true struggle lies.

Stay calm.

Don't let fear, anger, or even well-meant enthusiasm become your master. Develop a spirit of confident self-control.

Focus on keeping communication open over the longer term.

This requires attentiveness. For the friend who delights in a rousing battle of the wits, a good-natured argument is just the way to ensure many more conversations with him or her. But for the friend who dislikes confrontation, gentleness and compassion must take pride of place, so that your friend will feel comfortable coming to you with more questions down the road.

Answer questions in the way your listener will find most helpful.

Apologetics books and websites are a treasure trove of replies to anti-Catholic arguments. Choose among them wisely.* Avoid insults and avoid stoking fears. Your goddess-worshiping Wiccan friend might instinctively (and enthusiastically) embrace the role of Mary and the saints, whereas your Bible-only Evangelical friend is likely to need that stumbling block removed with precision and care, in order to clear up deeply entrenched misunderstandings. The most helpful answers will take into account your listener's background and current beliefs.

Don't make stuff up.

Know what you don't know. If you aren't sure of the answer to a question, say, "I'm not sure. Can I get back to you on that?"

---

* One of my go-tos is the *Handbook of Christian Apologetics* by Peter Kreeft and Ronald K. Tacelli, which is intellectually rigorous but generally charitable in its outlook.

Remember the goal.

Hint: the goal is not to prove how great you are at winning debates. It's to help souls grow closer to God. You "win" your argument only if your listener is thereby brought closer to Jesus Christ in the Catholic Faith.

Sometimes Apologetics Is Not the Answer

Sometimes a question, often a very targeted and virulent question, is a hurting heart wrapped in battle disguise. There is a time and a place for cool-headed, logical discussions of the problem of evil. But often what looks like an apologetics question is not a request for information at all but a request for reassurance and support.

When people are hurting, what they usually want to hear is this:

- Your pain is real and valid.
- You don't deserve to be treated this way.
- There are people in your life who want to help you.
- There is hope.
- You are loved — so very loved.

Here are some common things people say when they are hurting, and what the question might really mean:

- "Why did God let my child die?"

Not asking: Could you please explain to me the history of original sin and the logical implications of radical freedom?

Is asking: Oh my God, I am in agony, and I don't know if I can survive this darkness. Can you do anything at all to reassure me I am not alone as I go through this indescribable hell?

- "How can I trust the Church when there are so many terrible priests and bishops?"

Not asking: Could you please explain to me the biblical proof of the church's hierarchy and the distinction between legitimate authority and moral actions?

Is asking: I am furious. I cannot trust the Catholic Church because, frankly, its leaders have proven themselves not to be trustworthy. How can I even function as a sane human being in an organization that has such corrupt leadership?

- "What happens if someone commits suicide?"

Not asking: Could you please give me a lesson on mortal versus venial sin?

Is asking: I am in terrible torment and despair. Please give me a shred of hope.

There are no easy answers to any of these questions. You will have to discern, and perhaps even ask outright, how best to help your suffering friend. Is quiet companionship and help with the laundry what is needed most? Sharing your experience with a similar struggle may be exactly what your friend needs in order to feel less alone, or it could make your friend feel as if his or her grief has been trivialized; with your prayerful listening and a supersize dose of humility, the Holy Spirit can guide you through the quicksand.

Rage, despair, and grief are emotions that can feel too big or too wretched for God. The simple fact of a human friendship that remains steadfast when your friend is incapable of tame emotions may be the single, fragile lifeline that proves over time that God has not left the room.

A skilled apologist has ears open for the question behind the question. Apologetics is one of many tools in our evangelizer's toolbox, but it is not the most important tool. When faced with a friend who is deeply hurting, our best answer is not a carefully crafted argument. Our best answer is a copious outpouring of raw, unflinching, compassionate love.

For Reflection

- Are you familiar with the idea of apologetics? Are you comfortable with answering questions about the Catholic Faith?
- Does apologetics come naturally to you? Are you the sort who never walks away from a good, rousing argument? Or do you prefer to avoid confrontation and uncomfortable topics?
- What kinds of questions or concerns do people you know tend to have about the Faith?
- Are there types of questions that are likely to come up in your ministry? (For example, if you work in a crisis pregnancy center, your clients might have questions related to sexuality or the sacraments of baptism and marriage.) How can you learn more about how to answer those questions?
- Who or what is your go-to resource when people bring you questions you don't know how to answer?

Saints for Evangelists
Saint Peter Martyr (April 6)

Apologetics has been used as a tool for evangelization by many saints, including luminaries such as Justin Martyr and Francis de Sales. Saint Peter of Verona, also known as Saint Peter Martyr (1206–1252), was a Dominican friar and priest noted for evangelizing both lukewarm Catholics and neo-gnostic Cathars, who were openly antagonistic toward Trinitarian Christianity. As a defender of orthodoxy, he at times held official positions in the Inquisition (which in the 1200s was considerably different than in later periods) and was noted in that role for declaring clemency for those accused of heresy. He sought in his sermons to inspire not only outward assent to the Faith but true change of heart and a life lived for Jesus Christ.

His preaching tours drew great crowds and inspired many conversions, and thus fueled the rage of certain Cathars who did not appreciate the effect of Peter's missionary work. They hired an assassin, who ambushed and killed Peter and a companion while they were traveling home from a mission.

13

Workplace Missionaries

Is it even legal to evangelize at the office? Of everyone you know, the people you work with are likely the ones you see for the most hours every week. What are appropriate ways to help your colleagues grow closer to Jesus Christ, and what are some major hazards to avoid?

Key Points

- Regional culture and the cultures of our workplaces will affect how we evangelize our colleagues.
- Our roles in our workplaces will determine what types of evangelizing activities are appropriate.
- In most workplaces, our efforts will focus on making others comfortable with the fact of the Catholic Faith, but how we do that will vary significantly.
- We should not hide behind our fears but should choose to evangelize prudently in whatever ways God opens up to us.

The three main persons who evangelized me at work, in order from least to most important, were my boss, my primary client, and the Holy Spirit. Set forth as an example, here is what each one did.

My boss had to be careful — not because our workplace was an anti-Christian environment, but because sound ethics means avoiding conflicts of interest. Remember what I said about proselytizing? If it had even seemed as if my boss were trying to pressure me into Christianity, his part would have ceased to be true evangelization. So, the number-one thing he did was pray for me. The second thing he did was be a good boss. The third thing he did was quietly, but not secretly, live out his Christian faith.

My client had the luxury of being the customer, and customers can get away with a lot. He could strike up conversations that touched on religious topics during the chit-chat before we got down to business. He could ask questions that let me tell him more about what I was thinking and where I was in my relationship with God. When the time came, he could openly pray with me and outright ask me if I wanted to take the plunge and formally accept the Christian faith.

The Holy Spirit put it all together. Here's some irony for you: The client who ushered me back into the Catholic Faith wasn't even Catholic. That's how workplace evangelization sometimes unrolls, because God knows there are constraints on workplace relationships. As we are sensitive to the Lord's promptings at work, we also need to be confident in his providential care. Our job is to do the tasks God gives us; God's job is to manage the rest.

Culture Matters

There's a time and a place — here's looking at you, Saint Sebastian — to step up boldly and risk everything for Jesus Christ. But let's imagine that your calling isn't to be almost, but not quite, shot to death with arrows; let's imagine God is calling you to evangelize your co-workers through a less dramatic route that involves holding on to gainful employment.

In this day and age, your regional, industry, and company cultures can all have a huge bearing on what prudent, effective evangelization will look like.

In academia, conservative viewpoints and traditional Christian religious belief are often strongly discriminated against. Your activity as an evangelist is partly dictated by your ability carefully to avoid the land mines of wokedness while not compromising your beliefs. Survive that, and you can live to talk about Jesus with those who are open to what you have to say.

In the tech industry and in many media outlets (among other industries), publicly espousing conservative political positions is incompatible with high-profile employment. Though Catholicism is not a political movement in the least, certain moral issues, such as the sanctity of marriage and of human life, are considered too right-wing to be socially acceptable. Evangelization that begins with common ground in concern for the poor, in self-sacrificial love, and in a quest for truth, beauty, and goodness may be a route with long-term staying power.

In some regions, public displays of faith are considered taboo. To pray in public (including grace before meals), to display religious objects, and to talk about one's faith are perceived as imposing on others. At times, simply disregarding cultural pressure and cheerfully doing as you please may be the secret to shattering the silence around questions of faith and getting people to relax and open up. Other times, it will require careful thought to determine how to share your faith in a way that is encouraging and comforting rather than overwhelming and intimidating. Praying the Litany of Humility may help you to avoid actions that are unintentionally perceived as holier-than-thou.

In the Bible Belt, culturally approved Christianity coincides with widespread anti-Catholicism. If you live in the Bible Belt, you might work at a company where religious art hangs on the walls, company events begin with an invocation, Bible-study offerings are posted in the break room, and the office Christmas party is a true Christmas party. You might bump into your boss at the local March for Life — but also, your boss might be the one at the March for Life handing out the tracts explaining why the Catholic Church is the Whore of Babylon. Oops. Beg for holy wisdom to help you discern whether you will do better to join forces with your Evangelical colleagues in a joint effort at sharing Mere Christianity or whether you should boldly decorate your desk with Our Lady of Guadalupe candles and be That Weird Catholic. Typically, there is a middle ground to be found.

In small companies, pay close attention. Get a good feel for what the owner and senior management are comfortable with, and find a way to share your faith respectfully with those constraints in mind.

General Rules for Workplace Evangelization
With such a wide variety of work environments, it's impossible to lay out a set of no-fail steps for evangelization. Some general principles, though, can guide you on how to proceed.

Your position matters.
If you are the employee, you can openly evangelize your boss; the client can openly evangelize the supplier. If you are the boss, in contrast, you must scrupulously avoid any appearance of tying employment decisions to employee religious practice. In working with customers, respect your employer's preferences, but don't hide behind imaginary restrictions out of false humility.

Do let others know that you are Catholic.
When and how you break the news will depend on your environment. As an employee at a school sponsored by a Baptist church, I didn't put distinctively Catholic imagery on my desk — but peo-

ple were always asking where I went to church, so all I had to do was answer the question.

The fact that you are Catholic may come up naturally. Perhaps you have on your car a bumper sticker advertising the Catholic school your child attends; perhaps someone notices your large family in your desktop photo and asks if you are Mormon; perhaps you slip out at lunch for Ash Wednesday services. In a few very hostile workplaces, it may be important to use discretion concerning your faith until you have established strong relationships with your colleagues.

Put religion on the table as a comfortable topic.

Once people know I am Catholic (it doesn't take long), the questions start coming in. I make sure to tell people explicitly that I don't mind difficult or weird questions and that no one has yet succeeded in offending me. In your workplace, look around and judge what kinds of religious expressions are generally acceptable. Is religious jewelry commonly worn? Do people post inspirational sayings above their desks? Are you likely to be invited to a wedding, a christening, a bar mitzvah, or another event at a colleague's place of worship? Cultivate an inner attitude of joy and delight in your faith, so that when someone asks you about your religion, you can answer with the same pleasure people use when talking about their pets, their grandchildren, or their new fishing boats.

Learn how to answer religious questions diplomatically.

The nice thing about the fullness of the truth is that all you have to do is answer the question — but if you aren't sure what to answer, respond, "That's an important question, and I want to make sure I answer you accurately. Can I get back to you on that?"

For certain socially charged questions posed in environments that are hostile to Christian morality, it may be necessary to reply along these lines: "As I'm sure you know, that is an area that can be very controversial among Christians. Let me assure you that my fundamental belief is that all people are made in the image and likeness of God, and that God loves all persons wholeheartedly. On the off chance you were concerned, please also be assured that I respect you as a person and as a colleague, and I challenge you to hold me accountable if you ever see me say or do anything that suggests otherwise."

This does not mean that you deny the truth or go along with the crowd. It is important, however, to avoid getting bogged down in debates about contentious topics that distract from the more pressing question of God's existence and his involvement in salvation history. Few will change their opinion on moral issues until after they have developed a disciple's relationship with Jesus Christ. In contrast, once someone has accepted Christ as Lord and Savior, the desire to understand moral teaching will follow.

Go as far as the Lord allows.
Depending on your workplace, you may be able to:

- discuss religious topics with your colleagues, including asking them about their relationships with God up to this point in their lives
- offer to pray for your colleagues or even host a prayer group with other Christians in your workplace
- provide religious books or pamphlets with more information about the Catholic Faith
- host a Bible study at the office or invite one or more colleagues to join you for a Bible study before or after work
- invite colleagues to join you for Mass during the workday

- invite colleagues to attend events at your parish, including coming to Mass with you on Sundays
- cultivate friendships with colleagues beyond the office

Remember that, in evangelization, your top three tools are prayer and fasting; listening; and building long-term relationships.

> **"While respecting the beliefs and sensitivities of all, we must first clearly affirm our faith in Christ, the one Savior of mankind, a faith we have received as a gift from on high, not as a result of any merit of our own. We say with Paul, 'I am not ashamed of the Gospel: it is the power of God for salvation to everyone who has faith' (Rom 1:16). Christian martyrs of all times — including our own — have given and continue to give their lives in order to bear witness to this faith, in the conviction that every human being needs Jesus Christ, who has conquered sin and death and reconciled mankind to God."**
>
> — Saint John Paul II, *Redemptoris Missio*, "On the Permanent Validity of the Church's Missionary Mandate," 1990

For Reflection

- How would you describe your workplace environment? In what ways is it supportive of your Catholic faith? In what ways is it hostile to your faith?
- What is your position at work? How does your position affect your ability to evangelize? To what extent are you

able to evangelize in ways others cannot? In what ways must you prayerfully step back and let God do the work?

- Are there areas where you are letting fear disguise itself as false prudence? What is one small, safe step you could take to share your faith at work?

- Which person whom you work with could use your prayers for a closer relationship with Jesus Christ? Commit to praying daily for that colleague, and also pray for an opportunity for God to allow you openly to help that person grow closer to Christ.

Saints for Evangelists

Saint Michael Hồ Đình Hy (May 22)

Saint Michael Hồ Đình Hy (1808–1857) was born to wealthy parents in Vietnam and made his living as a silk trader. He married another Christian and had five children. Because of the persecution of Christians at the time, including the outlawing of Catholic priests, he and his family practiced their faith in private. When his son asked to become a priest, Saint Michael sent him to Indonesia, where his son could study for the seminary in comparative safety.

Saint Michael was appointed superintendent of the royal silk mills, an official position that involved travel on royal business. He used his position to ferry missionaries through Vietnam discreetly and safely. With his wealth, he provided for the poor and was known for his mercy and self-sacrifice on behalf of those caught up in difficult situations. After being denounced by a political enemy, he was eventually arrested for practicing Christianity. He was imprisoned, tortured, and beheaded.

14

Street Evangelization

Street preaching? Knocking on doors? Are these things that Catholics do? Well, yes, but maybe not quite as you fear. As Catholics, we have a hard time getting outside the walls of our parish churches or diocesan ministries — but going out is not optional in the command to "go out and make disciples."

Key Points

- We must leave our parishes and go out in search of the lost sheep who will never find us if we stay safely at home.
- Effective street evangelization is always respectful and always responsive to the individuals in front of us.
- Whether setting up shop in the streets or going door-to-door, the primary work will consist of prayer and active listening.
- Plan for follow-up with the people you meet, both in returning regularly to your mission

location and being ready to receive your new
friends in your parish.

Sometimes it seems as if we interpret the Great Commission to
mean, "If you build it, they will come." There are indeed places
where parishes are packed and congregations are pressed to build
larger and larger buildings. Unfortunately, this feeling of parishes
busting at the seams is often an illusion, created by a shortage of
priests combined with an influx of Catholics from other regions.
In other areas, old church buildings are virtually empty, parishes
are being closed, and sacred art is sold off to sunbelt congregations or private buyers.

Meanwhile, even in regions where church attendance is
strong, we see a curious phenomenon at older parishes: The Catholics often drive in from across town. In the vast majority of cases, people still live in the vicinity of our closing parishes — they
just aren't Catholic.

It Is Our Job

Having been raised Catholic doesn't mean that a person will stay
that way. In its "Religious Landscape Study of Americans," Pew
Research Center found that about 40 percent of those raised Catholic no longer "identify" as Catholic.[*] Keep in mind that someone
who "identifies" as Catholic might or might not attend Mass or
believe in Catholic teaching — as many pastors and catechists
can attest. But looking only at this very weakest level of faith, to
say that Catholics have a 60 percent retention rate is overly opti-
mistic. What Pew Research has found is that each new generation
is more and more likely to leave the Church. Among millennials

---

* Michael Lipka, "5 Key Findings about the Changing U.S. Religious
Landscape," Pew Research Center, May 12, 2015, https://www.pewforum.
org/2015/05/12/chapter-2-religious-switching-and-intermarriage/.

polled in 2014, only 50 percent continued to call themselves Catholic into adulthood. The decline is steady and continuing. A separate set of more recent data show a 3 percent drop between 2009 and 2019 in the percentage of U.S. adults identifying as Catholic; of those, the percentage of Hispanic respondents identifying as Catholic dropped by 10 percent, and the percentage of millennials identifying as Catholic dropped by 9 percent.[†] Informal polls of Catholics I meet bear these statistics out.

Thus, we know from experience that what we are doing in our homes and parishes is not sufficient to pass on the Catholic Faith to the next generation. What we overlook is that the departure of those raised Catholic is directly related to our abandoning our mission to go out and make disciples: Why should our children bother with a religion that we ourselves consider optional?

By our decision not to evangelize beyond the walls of our parishes, we are saying that it just doesn't matter whether the people in our community discover the Catholic Faith.

That Crazy Guy on the Corner

Most of us want to be normal people who get along. We don't enjoy making waves. We don't enjoy making other people uncomfortable. We definitely don't want to be that nutcase on the street corner shouting about damnation, and we really don't want to be those obnoxious door-to-door religion salesmen either.

Good news: God is not asking you to do any of that.

Unsettling news: Those people who are getting it all wrong are also getting a few things right.

To understand the difference, we have to remember our guiding principle: Evangelization is always done one soul at a time.

---

† Pew Research Center, "In U.S., Decline of Christianity Continues at Rapid Pace," Pew Research Center, October 17, 2019 https://www.pewforum.org/2019/10/17/in-u-s-decline-of-christianity-continues-at-rapid-pace/.

"Like St. Paul, every preacher devoted to the
salvation of souls should be first of all so zealous
for God's service as to feel no concern about
who his hearers are to be, what success he will
have, or what fruits he is to reap. He should
have an eye not to his own advantage but to
God's glory."
— Pope Benedict XV, *Humani Generis Redemptionem*,
"On Preaching the Word of God," 1917

What Does Effective Street Preaching Look Like?

You probably know a couple of famous Catholic street preachers — there might even be the statue of one in your yard. Saint Francis of Assisi and Saint Dominic were nuts, and if you don't believe me, ask their parents. What kind of son of well-to-do parents gives up a good living to go out and make waves? These were Catholic communities. Why couldn't these troublesome boys leave people to pray in peace, with no sermonizing or interfering?

The answer is that Francis and Dominic both heard the call to carry out the Great Commission in their distinctive ways. They both loved their neighbors too much to leave them stewing in a lukewarm faith.

Fast-forward seven hundred years, and meet another Catholic street preacher, this one in mid-1900s England. Frank Sheed was part of a group of laypeople who would go out to the city parks and speak to passersby, often responding to the arguments of hecklers, which was the accepted custom of the time and place. It was crazy, but it was the kind of crazy the local community enjoyed and allowed.

Fast-forward another fifty or seventy years. What do successful Catholic street preachers do today?

First of all, they pray. Just like Saint Francis of Assisi, Saint Dominic, Frank Sheed, and countless other evangelists through the ages, ordinary Catholics who go out into the streets today begin their work in front of the Blessed Sacrament.

Secondly, they speak and listen to the individuals they meet. Many parish lay evangelists today report that the most successful format is to set up a table at a community event, such as a festival or a street market, abiding by whatever rules the event organizers have in place. The lay evangelists will bring a selection of useful literature, such as brochures answering questions about the Catholic Faith. Depending on the area, there may be suitable gifts to hand out, such as prayer cards or rosaries. (In some regions, such gifts would not be well received.)

The evangelist will ask visitors two main questions:

1.   How can I pray for you?
2.   What questions do you have?

The evangelist will listen carefully and ask follow-up questions in order to learn more. Before the person leaves, the evangelist will ask whether the person would like to pray with him or her.

And that's it.

Not too scary after all.

Ding-Dong, Jesus Is Knocking

When Catholic lay evangelists go door-to-door, the most common approaches are similar. Sometimes groups go out specifically to invite the residents of the parish neighborhood to an upcoming event, such as a Christmas program or Easter egg hunt. Other times they simply go out to meet the neighbors and pray for them.

A typical encounter would begin with this: "Hi, we're from Our Lady the Good Neighbor parish. We were wondering, how can we pray for you today?"

Asking for prayer requests is a good way to find out how to pray for your neighbors. It also allows those who answer the door to share what is on their hearts, talk about struggles with their faith, or perhaps offer an encouraging word to the parish missionaries.

When going door-to-door, it is a good idea to bring information about parish or diocesan ministries that can help with practical needs, including at least one catch-all contact person, such as someone at a Catholic Charities office who can connect callers with other community services.

Street Work Is the Beginning, Not the End

Thinking through the pyramid of evangelization encounters from chapter 9, on corporal works of mercy, the vast majority of your encounters in street initiatives are going to be those "middle moments": those brief encounters that may end up playing an important role in a long chain of events leading someone closer to Jesus Christ. That alone makes street work worthwhile. For priests who are able to set up a mobile confessional at community events, the work will be life changing.

But remember that the fullness of evangelization takes place through long-term relationships. How do you make that happen?

Same bat time, same bat channel.

Come back again on a regular schedule. Set up your table every week at the farmer's market, every month at the craft fair, or every summer at the pie festival. If you visit door-to-door, make a monthly routine of visiting the same neighborhoods (first Saturdays, second Sundays, and so forth), and leave a polite but not overbearing note for neighbors who welcomed your visit in the past but were not there on the follow-up visit.

Accept follow-up invitations when appropriate.

Use your common sense concerning personal safety, but in particular for neighbors who are unable to come to the local parish due to illness or other limitations, see if you can arrange a way to come back to visit more often if asked to do so. (A parish phone ministry can be a good way to follow up with homebound community members as well.) If a visitor to your evangelization table at a community event requests that you send a speaker or that you consider a joint event with another community organization, at least look into the possibility.

Have a schedule of upcoming events.

Have a schedule of upcoming events, and have a pen ready, so you can circle events of specific interest to the person you meet. In ministry areas where your parish is shorthanded, include events at other parishes as well. For example, if most events at your parish aren't a good fit for young, working professionals, but Saint Collegius in the next town does a pile of such events, have that information on hand. Remember, the goal isn't parish growth. Your goal is the personal growth of the person you are getting to know. Not everyone you meet will be best helped at your home parish.

Involve newcomers in your parish community.

A Catholic parish can be the loneliest place in the world. It does little good to go out into the streets proclaiming the Good News if those who arrive in your pews are going to be ignored and abandoned. All of us in the parish — not just the welcoming committee — need to become masters at recognizing newcomers, greeting them, striking up conversations, and inviting them to get involved in parish life. I know that's a tall order for those of us who are shy, and we don't need to go to the other extreme and scare away all the introverts. An important conversation every parish needs to have is on how to welcome and include those who are hardest to include, whether due to temperament or some other factor that makes joining in parish life a daunting prospect.

Evangelization Outposts

Going out to the world can also take the form of establishing permanent places of encounter through businesses or nonprofits that are explicitly Catholic and openly seek to host conversations on the Faith. Examples include Catholic bookstores in secular shopping centers; coffee shops, restaurants, or bars; dance or martial arts studios; tutoring or education centers; book clubs; gyms and recreation centers. Chapter 16, "Crafting Parish Events," includes many ideas for initiatives that could work for an evangelizing outpost in the community rather than as a parish event.

Many Catholics own businesses, and these can and should play a role in evangelization, but owners and employees need to discern their proper roles. What makes an evangelizing outpost distinctive is the intentional creation of an explicit invitation for visitors to bring up religion as an accepted topic and know that an employee or host is ready and willing to answer spiritual questions.

Creating More Than Just Busy Parishioners

What is the point of street evangelization? The goal is to lead those we meet through all five thresholds of faith in Jesus Christ: trust, curiosity, openness, seeking, and full-fledged discipleship.

Sometimes in street work, we will have just a single pinpoint encounter, a quick brush with the grace of God in action. Other times, a relationship will blossom that will involve walking someone through all five thresholds out on the street, in a series of ongoing encounters that occur over months or years. In yet other cases, the person we meet in street work may come quickly to the parish doors — but that doesn't mean our work is done.

It only means that the walk through the five thresholds has, at least in part, moved off the street and into the parish. In the chapters ahead, we'll see how we can make our parishes ready to receive newcomers fruitfully, regardless of where they are along the spiritual path of conversion.

For Reflection

- Have you had a positive encounter with a street or door-to-door evangelist? What negative encounters have you had? What was the difference?
- What kind of street evangelization would be most suited to your personality? Do you enjoy talking with people? Helping people? Getting into deep conversations or just shooting the breeze?
- Which people in your area will never meet the Church unless someone goes to them? Where do those people live or work? What time of day would they be most open to taking a few minutes to talk with a friendly listener?
- What would it take for you to be comfortable with evangelizing in public? If you were to create your ideal outreach team, who would be on it? Where would you go, and what would you do?

For More Information: Street Evangelization Ministries Worth Knowing

There are more Catholic evangelists taking to the streets than you may realize. Here are three groups who specialize in going out "to the hedgerows" and reaching those who would not otherwise encounter the Catholic Faith.

Saint Paul Street Evangelization (streetevangelization.com) is an apostolate dedicated to training and equipping lay Catholics to go out into the streets and evangelize in a prayerful, nonconfrontational manner, along the lines laid out in this chapter.

Christ in the City (christinthecity.com) is a missionary society based in Denver, Colorado, whose model is building lasting friendships with the homeless residents of the cities they serve.

Volunteers are young adults who live in community and divide their time between prayer, formation, and service among the homeless in their city.

Street Pastors (streetpastors.org) is an interdenominational Christian initiative founded in London, England, whose mission is to minister to those out on the streets at night. Volunteers (including many Catholics) are vetted by their local churches and trained to go out in teams of men and women to care for, listen to, and help people who are on the streets. They are often called in to provide help in crises related to late-night drinking at bars or pubs.

Saints for Evangelists

Saint Pedro Calungsod (April 2)

Saint Pedro Calungsod (1654–1672), a native of the Philippines, was one of several teenagers chosen to join the mission of Blessed Diego Luis de San Vitores to what are now the Mariana Islands. After the young men were trained as catechists, they set out to evangelize the native Chamorro people; at Father Diego's instruction, the priests and lay catechists of the mission went unarmed. Conditions on the islands were physically difficult and socially fraught. Initially, the missionaries were welcomed by local authorities, but it quickly became apparent that Christian beliefs were in direct conflict with traditional social customs, morals, and religious beliefs.

Pedro persisted in his work of traveling the islands as a catechist, converting hearts through the example of his profound faith and his purity. Rumor spread, however, that infants were getting sick and dying because the missionaries used poisoned water in baptisms. (Disease carried to the islands by Spanish colonists would, in time, kill a vast portion of the indigenous population, so the fear was not unfounded, even though the rumor was patently false.) As a result, a local chief abandoned Christianity and was furious when his wife, still a Christian, had their newborn baby baptized. Enraged, he and an accomplice attacked and killed Pedro and Father Diego with spears.

15

Hospitality

Is your door always open? Is yours the place people come just to hang out? Human beings are made to love and be loved, to know and be known. We will do almost anything to satisfy our need for connection with others. Let's move beyond the parish potluck or the carefully orchestrated dinner party and figure out how to practice some serious hospitality.

Key Points

- Hospitality is more than just being friendly. Hospitality involves a personal desire to welcome the other into your life.
- We must plan for hospitality so that the demands of existing friendships and obligations don't sabotage our good intentions.
- We must never take advantage of so-called friendship to treat another person as an object.
- Parish hospitality includes opening the doors to full participation in the life of the community

for disciples with disabilities.
- Hospitality is the natural outflowing of authentic love. If I am struggling with welcoming others, it is my heart that needs work first.

Some years ago, I experienced an illness that came on suddenly and resolved slowly. As someone who had previously assisted at Mass nearly daily, I was grateful when I recovered enough to be dropped off at the church door on a Saturday evening, find a quiet corner where I could sit leaning against the wall, and pray along silently as the congregation worshiped around me with the customary Catholic gymnastics. At that time, any conversation at all was extremely difficult for me, and it would remain a strain for several years.

Fortunately, I am Catholic, so the solution to the conversation problem was simple: attend at the neighboring parish. If there is one thing you can almost count on, it is that no one will speak to a stranger at a Catholic church.

What Is Hospitality?

Hospitality is the opposite of never speaking to strangers, but it is something greater and deeper than mere friendliness. I have talked to a number of non-Catholic Christians who lamented as they left their current congregation that although everyone was outwardly very friendly, friendship was always superficial. After years of trying to build deep friendships without success, they decided to look elsewhere for a true welcome.

Hospitality requires two things:

1. I must be at home.
2. I must want you to join in the life of my home.

To be at home means I have a sense of ownership and belonging in my sphere, whatever it might be. If I am sitting at a table at the coffee shop and there is an empty chair across from me, in a certain sense I am at home at my little table. That empty seat across from me is "mine," and by custom, if someone wants to sit there or borrow the empty chair, that person should ask me first. It is a violation of social norms for a stranger to sit down across the table from another stranger without first asking permission.

I am at home in a circle of friends if I feel free to invite others to come chat with us as my friends and I stand on the pavement in front of the school waiting for our children to come out of practice. I am at home in cohosting a party (regardless of its location) if I feel free to hand out invitations.

Welcome Is More Than Courtesy

Now, in all these situations where I am at home, I might find myself courteously enduring someone else's presence without truly wanting that person to join in this part of my life. In a crowded coffee shop, I might allow another customer to sit across from me, even though I have no intention of forming any kind of relationship with that person. Waiting for my child to come out of practice, I might make small talk with another parent, lest I seem rude or perhaps in order to solve some logistical matter concerning an upcoming game. I might politely tolerate the intrusion of an unwanted "friend" into a social gathering because refusing to extend the invitation would give needless offense.

Hospitality is not the polite acceptance of an unavoidable or expedient presence. Hospitality is choosing to welcome someone into my sphere because I truly want that person there, and I want him or her to share, in some way, life as part of my home.

In the coffee shop, I invite you to sit down because I welcome your companionship. Waiting for practice to get out, I strike up a conversation because I am interested to hear how you are doing and what you have to say today. I invite you to the party because

I look forward to having you join in the celebration — there's a sense that your presence makes the day more complete and more festive.

Hospitality in Parish Life

For a parish to practice hospitality, both components must be present. As a member of my parish, I must feel, in some sense, at home in my parish. The extent to which I feel at home will dictate how much hospitality I can extend. Am I comfortable only representing myself as a private individual standing outside on the playground after Mass, watching my children play? Then I might feel free (if I work up the courage) to introduce myself as one parent to another, but my welcome will be more like two travelers on a voyage abroad. We might compare notes on how to navigate the world of the parish, but without a sense that it is ours.

A ministry sometimes flounders because the sense of ownership is too restricted. Do members of the Bible study feel free to invite others, or do they feel (rightly or wrongly) that newcomers need to email the leader and find out if someone else can join?

Beyond a sense of ownership, though, parishioners and staff must want a relationship with those being welcomed. Sometimes it seems as if Catholics live by mottos such as "Stick to your clique" or "A stranger is just a headache you've never met." It is one thing to put out coffee and doughnuts and feel that everyone who so chooses may walk over after Mass and have a bite to eat while they speak to their people. It is another to put out coffee and doughnuts, not just planning to greet newcomers politely, but hoping to form new, lasting friendships that will involve praying for one another by name and serving together in many ways throughout years of missionary work together.

Obstacles to Forming New Friendships

One year, a friend and I had to make a rule for ourselves as we stood on the playground after Mass: no talking to each other.

The temptation was strong. On any given Sunday, we might have all kinds of news to catch up on. But we both knew well the loneliness that comes from being ignored in the parish social scene. I could think of times when I stood with a cup of coffee in the parish hall, looking at circles of backs turned my way, as everyone in the room was too busy catching up with their buddies to notice the lonely newcomer.

Friendship is often an obstacle to hospitality!

I can think of another time when I sat at a parish meet-and-greet and found myself focused entirely on answering the pressing questions of one of the members of my Bible study. I glanced across the table at some parents I was eager to know better, but it simply wasn't possible to hold two conversations at once. I had to choose whether to push off my student's time-sensitive questions or to postpone getting to know new friends. Discipleship can be an obstacle to hospitality!

There are no perfect answers to quandaries like these, but there are two things that can help. The first is planning ahead for the reality of human limitations and attempting to have more welcomers at a parish event than we think will be needed. The second is to build up our parish community life so that more time is built into the week for friendships and discipleship conversations. If nothing else, a humble recognition of the obstacles to forming new friendships can open our eyes to insights on how to overcome them.

Getting Over the Hump

One of the great challenges Catholic parishes face in creating a culture of hospitality is getting over the embarrassment of not knowing friend from stranger. There you are after Mass, standing around at coffee, working up your courage to try this welcoming business. You see a likely candidate, that lovely couple who sat behind you at Mass today. You put on a big smile and march on over and extend your hand. "Hi!" you say, and introduce yourself. "What brings you to our parish today?"

And that's when your "new visitors" say, "Well, we moved here for work in 1993. We've been sitting three rows behind you for the last ten years. I used to be your daughter's CCD teacher."

Oops. And you know that this could happen in many parishes.

As with all obstacles to evangelization, we have to clothe ourselves in humility and admit that our parish is going to have to go through a transition period as we get the hang of becoming friends. As a parish, we'll need to create some intentional ways of causing parishioners to meet each other — not just to view each other or eat the same casserole, but to get introduced and spend time learning more about one another. We might have to start wearing name tags at parish mixers. We might have to host parish mixers. Above all, we'll need to announce a ban on social awkwardness: No more feeling shy about asking someone's name thirty-seven times. No more blushing if you have to ask whether someone is new or it's just a fresh haircut. We cannot let pride keep us from knowing one another.

Evangelizing Hospitality

When we practice Christian hospitality, whether at home, in our parishes, or in the mission field, we are not seeking to proselytize. It is not our goal to gather up new Catholics because we want to increase the collection or add a notch in our belt for each time our excellent work at putting out doughnuts and casseroles results in another baptism.

Hospitality is the act of truly welcoming another person to join in our lives. Why do we welcome the stranger? Because it is our destiny. Human beings are made for perfect communion with God and with one another. In this broken world, differences in opinion or personality might hamper that communion, but we are not made for brokenness.

Hospitality works as an approach to evangelization because human beings long to know and be known, to love and be loved. I say that cautiously, however, because we must not use relationships as a way of using people into the church. One of the most chilling aspects of accounts of clerical sexual abuse is that, almost to a one, the criminal uses the target's need for love, and need for a relationship with God, to prey on vulnerabilities and twist the truth into a series of heinous lies. It is in no way our mission as evangelists to use relationships in order to get people to do things for us, no matter how good our goals or how beneficial the things we want done may be.

True evangelization, in contrast to proselytizing, is the natural outflowing of authentic love. Through acts of hospitality at home, at work, in public places, and in our parishes, we seek to welcome and create a place for those whom God has sent to share with us both this fleeting mortal existence and the never-ending joy of eternal life.

Are Catholics with Disabilities Welcome at Your Parish?

There's one more thing we need to talk about.

In 1978, the U.S. Catholic bishops wrote, "For most Catholics the community of believers is embodied in the local parish. The parish is the door to participation for individuals with disabilities, and it is the responsibility of the pastor and lay leaders to make sure that this door is always open."* Forty years later, the doors are still — sometimes literally — locked for many Catholics

---

* United States Catholic Conference, *Pastoral Statement of U.S. Catholic Bishops on Persons with Disabilities* (Washington, DC: United States Catholic Conference, 1978), 5.

with disabilities.

In a few short minutes of conversation, Catholic author Rebecca Frech (mother of WCMX champion Ella Frech) and deaf Catholic author Emily DeArdo (*Living Memento Mori*) compiled a short list of areas in which Catholic parishes often fall short in making sure all parishioners can participate in parish life. Some of these adaptations are astonishingly simple:

- microphones (yes, just turning on the mic and using it makes a difference for a hearing-impaired listener)
- telecoil systems
- wheelchair-accessible confessionals
- face-to-face confession (for those who need visual contact to understand speech)
- Braille missals
- large-print missals
- plugs in the nave for power chairs and portable oxygen concentrators
- adult-size changing tables
- power buttons for doors
- bathroom stalls large enough for a wheelchair to turn around in

I've been thrilled to note how a parish near me seems to be constantly making small improvements to be more hospitable in this area. There are many heartening examples of parishes going the extra mile to be truly welcoming to all comers. Aimee O'Connell, an autistic Catholic who oversees the Mission of Saint Thorlak, shared with me how creating a sensory-friendly worship space at her parish made Mass attendance possible for the first time for many parishioners.

Many Catholics mentioned that all-inclusive hospitality doesn't have to cost a cent. Cathy Lins, in discussing with me ways to meet the needs of visitors and parishioners with mental illness or psychological trauma, shared the importance of normalizing belonging. When discussing the Sacrament of Anointing of the Sick, we should mention that serious mental illness may be a reason to be anointed; in the prayers of the faithful, we should intercede for those struggling with addiction or healing from past abuse; in the reminder to contact the parish if a hospital visit is needed, we should note that priests or extraordinary ministers of the Eucharist can visit psych wards and addiction treatment centers.

A simple heads-up can do wonders. Theodore Seeber reported that knowing which instruments will be used for music in the liturgy is important in planning for those with sensory-processing disorders. "I have autism. ... I love the folk Mass at my parish, but on a weekend with a migraine that trumpet is like a knife through the skull. Violins also get to me." That's not a need the music ministry would necessarily be able to anticipate, but once a parishioner mentions the need, it's a very simple situation to accommodate.

Unfortunately, stories of exclusion abound. Several parents told of having to ask around at multiple parishes to find one that would assist in preparing their children with disabilities for the sacraments; Catholics with celiac, gluten allergy, or chemical allergies (which can include incense) report facing outright disbelief from pastoral staff who ascribed their medical condition to hysteria or lack of faith. Multiple Catholic teens mentioned that their parish youth-group activities were systematically unwelcoming to students with physical disabilities.

One couple explained how they were never included in parish outings due to needing wheelchair access:

> While we could easily attend Sunday Mass (weekday Masses were inaccessible), parish events were

not always inclusive. The parish went to a Major
League Baseball game in our city. We signed up
to go, but the parish traveled together on a bus —
except us (we had to make our own way to the
stadium) — and once there, we were seated in an
entirely different section of the ballpark from our
parish. Not much of a "parish" event for us — and
this was a typical example of our experiences, not
an exception. We signed up to go on retreat with
the parish — but the retreat house was inaccessible. Over the years, just about every event held
away from the parish buildings was inaccessible
or at least very difficult.

Sometimes attempts at providing support go awry, such as having in a diocese an office that will assist you with getting an ASL
interpreter for Mass but puts you in touch with someone who
assumes you can hear well enough to use the telephone. Emily
DeArdo writes, "When it says in the bulletin, 'Call this person
for reservations,' I just throw my hands up! At least tell me if I
can text!"

Multiple contact options (telephone, text, email, visiting the
parish office) allow as many parishioners as possible access to a
given ministry of the parish. Keep in mind that more than one
person can be a go-to contact for the same event, rather than
requiring a single parishioner to manage all possible modes of
communication.

One of the chief challenges many Catholics face, whether for
financial, physical, or scheduling reasons, is simply getting to the
parish. If it's possible to make the trip only once a week (at most),
then any parishioner needs must be met at that time or go unmet.
Special-needs parent Mary Hathaway emphasized that offering
confession and anointing of the sick immediately before or after

regularly scheduled Masses is a lifesaver for Catholics with significant caregiving responsibilities.

"The Church founded by the Redeemer is one, the same for all races and all nations. Beneath her dome, as beneath the vault of heaven, there is but one country for all nations and tongues; there is room for the development of every quality, advantage, task and vocation which God the Creator and Savior has allotted to individuals as well as to ethnical communities."
— Pope Pius XI, *Mit Brennender Sorge*, "On the Church and the German Reich," 1937

Be Led by the Person You're Trying to Assist

Good intentions don't change the reality that none of us are omniscient. I'll be honest: I had never heard of adult changing tables before researching this chapter. Once informed, it made perfect sense, but how do we get to the point of being fully informed?

Begin by going to the experts. If your goal is to make it possible for someone to attend Mass, receive the sacraments, lead or participate in parish ministries, grow in his or her faith, and generally become a regular part of parish life, the person you are trying to include is the best expert on his or her needs.

Technologies change. Individuals vary. Working with the experts pays off financially, because you eliminate the guesswork on what types of investments are truly helpful. If you consult the experts early enough in the planning process for regularly planned special events or construction projects, there will likely be no cost difference at all in the barrier-free approach.

Budgeting for Accommodations

There's a misconception that it's somehow too expensive for a parish to make its facilities usable for all Catholics. In taking into account budgeting decisions, there are several factors to consider:

- Have we installed all the low-tech, low-cost solutions available to us?
- Have we identified manageable upgrades and made a plan to carry them out?
- Are we building a wish list for our next budget cycle?

When you are serious about opening the doors, it is usually possible to cut a planned expense elsewhere to pay for minor upgrades or to find a parishioner willing to donate the needed supplies and carpentry or engineering skills. When the full solution is out of the budget, a partial solution may be enough to get by temporarily, until full funding can be allocated.

Play to Win at the Communication Game
Disability, whether physical, cognitive, or psychological, is but a subset of the larger problem of parishioners who face barriers to participation in parish life. What are some ways we can get the hospitality ball rolling before someone gives up in frustration and leaves?

- Aggressively and preemptively work through common barriers to participation at Mass, and post pertinent information on the parish website. It shouldn't require much more than a few clicks for visitors to know how the parish accommodates situations that may seem rare and yet affect vast numbers of people.
- Use signage to communicate the availability of accommodations and their correct use. (Is that

a nursery or a sensory-friendly worship space? What line do I get into if I need a low-gluten host? Where is the fragrance-free seating area? How do I let the priest sitting in the confessional know I can't hear and need face-to-face confession?)

- Have a phone number, an email address, and an online contact form so visitors can communicate unusual needs in advance of a parish visit and receive a timely reply.

- Train parish staff and volunteers, including ordinary parishioners who are willing to help in a pinch, in first aid and safety procedures, including mental-health first aid.

- Use signage and audio announcements to direct parishioners to the point person (an usher? a deacon? a designated volunteer?) for needs that arise before, during, or after Mass.

- Choose a staff member who is good at listening, welcoming, and logistics to be the lead on solutions that require longer-term follow-up.

- Communicate responses. Once you receive a request for assistance and respond to that request, add it to your parish routines, and publicize that routine using signage, the website, announcements, and staff and volunteer training.

- Make responding to individual needs part of the parish culture.

It's impossible to anticipate every single difficulty that will ever come up in parish life. The good news is that practicing active hospitality causes our welcoming muscles to get stronger and more flexible.

Is it normal for people with nonroutine situations to be welcomed at your parish? Is authentic hospitality so commonplace that it would be downright laughable for someone to fear butting heads with entrenched bureaucracy? Would, say, a parent whose child can't complete the standard procedure for sacramental prep be absolutely confident that the parish staff would consider it a normal part of their job to figure out an alternative?

The key to hospitality is in our hearts. Do we believe that what we do at church is truly necessary? Is the work of our parish or our ministry truly worthwhile for all people? Sometimes the reason we don't install that telecoil system or unlock the door at the top of the wheelchair ramp is that we honestly don't believe that what we do matters. We don't make sacramental prep available at no cost, or work our schedule so shift workers can attend Mass, because we don't feel it's honestly all that big a deal. It's fine for those who can come, but others shouldn't worry too much about missing out.

Evangelists don't believe that. Evangelists believe that God intends to use our parishes as the means of offering eternal life to the whole human race.

For Reflection

- Are you good at making friends? What kinds of social situations are most comfortable for you? What are your strengths and weaknesses as a friend?
- When has someone showed genuine hospitality toward you? What did that person do to make you feel welcome? How did that change your experience?
- What obstacles do you face in welcoming others into your life? (This could include health problems, work schedules, family responsibilities, or any other factors). How do you see God working even in the limitations he

sets in your life?

- Think about a common situation in your parish, your ministry, or your everyday life when you have the chance to speak to other people. How can you, personally, welcome new friendships and build up existing friendships during that time?
- Are there situations in which a team approach to improving hospitality could take your outreach efforts to the next level?

Saints for Evangelists

Venerable Pierre Toussaint

Venerable Pierre Toussaint (1766–1853) was born in slavery in Haiti and was taken by his owners to New York City in 1787. There he learned the trade of hairdressing, and after he was freed in 1807, his business flourished. He and his wife, Juliette, used their wealth to help others, including sheltering orphans and refugees and assisting immigrants in getting settled. Pierre and Juliette purchased the freedom of slaves, helped build the first school for black children in New York City, and funded the Oblate Sisters of Providence. During a major epidemic, Pierre entered quarantined neighborhoods in order to tend to the sick.

The care of Pierre and Juliette for those in need crossed all social barriers, and his generosity and charity were admired by all who knew him. After his cause for canonization was opened, his remains were moved from Old St. Patrick's (which he helped to build) to the present St. Patrick's Cathedral.

16

Crafting Parish Events

If someone in your community wanted to find out more about what the Catholic Church is really like, how easy would it be? Let's look at some types of events that you or your parish might host and how you can make them places for strangers to meet Catholics and meet the Church.

Key Points

- Low-threat opportunities to meet the Church allow members of our wider community to encounter Catholics and ask questions about the Catholic Faith.
- If we want to evangelize, we need to make sure our events are designed to allow for relationship building and spiritual follow-up.
- Different events serve different purposes. Given limited resources, we need to make hard decisions about how to prioritize parish efforts.
- One-soul-at-a-time thinking is the key ingredient

in putting together effective evangelizing events.

If I want to make a friend, I start with an invitation: Come join me; I've got something going on that I think you'll enjoy. Spending time together is the only way for people to get to know one another. The same is true of inviting the people in our communities to get to know the Catholic Church.

Let's look at some common types of events that Catholic parishes are using to encourage the curious to come and see. The few examples I give here, organized by the kind of needs they meet, are just a smattering of the many creative ways parishes are creating bridges of welcome. After we've considered some options, we'll talk about the difference between a true evangelizing initiative and simply getting someone to show up and play along until he or she decides to move on.

Events for Building Friendships

Let's start with a few events that all have one thing in common: They aren't inherently Christian events; they are just ordinary things people like to do. All of these can be great activities for parishioners, because they allow us to strengthen our communities by doing together what we would otherwise do elsewhere. If the events are run by disciples who make sure to maintain a wholesome, upbeat atmosphere, they will appeal to families and others seeking a clean, safe place to unwind and relax.

- Rummage sales
  Everybody's got clutter, and everyone could stand to save a few dollars by buying second-hand. A parish-sponsored yard sale could serve as a fundraiser for a cause that has general community support (such as funding a food pantry), or it could be an opportunity for individuals to set

up tables and try to sell a few things to fill some holes in their household budgets.

- Parish festivals
  In some parts of the country, the annual parish festival is a major community event or parish fundraiser. Whether you've been hosting a festival every year since 1856 or are considering it for the first time, the idea is that everyone can come and play games, jump in the bouncy house, eat deep-fried everything, and relax with friends.

- Craft clubs
  We might envision a bunch of old women sitting around, quilting or knitting, but arts and crafts are popular with people of all ages. Craft clubs can be a great opportunity for building intergenerational relationships, especially if the scheduling and child-care arrangements make it possible for working or single parents to attend.

- Sports
  As much as church staff complain about having to compete with sports, the reality is that a lot of people have bodies they enjoy challenging with athletic activities. Parents (and teachers!) want a way for energetic children to work off some energy in an era when few families have labor-intensive farm chores for their kids. The three areas where churches can fill the greatest gaps are in entry-level sports for older kids (school and club teams become highly competitive at younger and younger ages), recreational leagues

for adults, and adaptive sports for athletes with disabilities.

One caution for pastors who sponsor these events is that general-interest activities will draw the enthusiasm of parishioners who are not necessarily disciples or whose faith is still very immature. Without being heavy-handed or needlessly rigid, and recognizing that pairing leaders on secular initiatives is a great way to mentor parishioners, it is important to provide strong moral leadership. It will do little good if the ladies are sharing notes on their favorite contraceptives as they piece together their quilt patterns, or the music blasting at the parish festival is one long ode to the pleasures of fornication. Before friendship-building initiatives can bear fruit, the parish itself must be evangelized.

Events for Piquing Curiosity

Friendship-building activities are great for building bridges of trust. When someone reaches the threshold of curiosity, we have an opportunity to reach out to the community by drawing on our vast wealth of historical and artistic treasures. Here are a few that parishes have used to good effect.

- Church or graveyard tours
  If your parish has historical, architectural, or artistic interest, guided or self-guided tours are a great way to present more information about the Faith. Historical cemeteries are of interest all year long, but graveyards of any vintage have potential as the setting for a well-presented All Hallow's Eve annual event.

- Concerts
  Musical events open to the public can take on a

variety of forms. Highly skilled musicians from your parish can perform sacred music for discerning audiences. Touring groups, such as the school chorus from a Catholic college, can offer better-quality concerts even if your parish is barely holding its head above water in the music department. And finally, your enthusiastic church choir, however amateur, can draw a fan base of friends and family who might not come to Mass on Sundays, but who will turn out for a Christmas-caroling event.

- Film festivals
  If you have a meeting room with adequate seating, a good large-screen television, and decent sound, all you have to do is pop the popcorn and hit Play. Events can range from family movies to demanding art-house cinema. Copyright rules vary by jurisdiction; Church Video License* provides affordable blanket licenses for churches hosting screenings of commercial films, subject to restrictions on admission fees and public advertising. Many Catholic videos are sold with a license for church screenings included, so contact the publisher for details.

    Your goals, your resources, and your audience will determine how your evangelizing event unrolls. Do you want to offer a weekly summer

---

* For U.S. licensing, see us.cvli.com. The same organization serves Canada at ca.ccli.com and the United Kingdom at uk.ccli.com, as well as many other countries around the world. Click on the country selector to learn the details of licenses available in your area.

kids' movie as a way for moms to be able to meet and chat in a parent break room? Do you want to show highbrow cinema and afterward host a rousing discussion that brings together the readers of *First Things* and the university art department?

What all of these types of events have in common is that the opportunity to make spiritual connections is definitely there. It is also possible, however, to put a lot of time and energy into evangelizing events of this type strictly as trust- or friendship-building efforts, neglecting the chance to raise deeper questions.

Events That Meet Serious Needs

"I was going through the worst time of my life, and the Church was not there for me." These are words we don't want to hear. As Catholics, we know, as a matter of dogma, that we live in a fallen world. People suffer. They struggle. When someone poses the question "Where is God in all my suffering?" we hope the answer will be, "He is down the street at the Catholic church."

- Programs for the divorced and for couples in struggling marriages
  The formal ministry DivorceCare is a nondenominational Evangelical (Protestant) program, but it is used by many Catholic parishes. The Surviving Divorce program (catholicsdivorce. com) by Catholic speaker Rose Sweet is a Catholic option. Retrouvaille (helpourmarriage.org) is a Catholic retreat for couples in struggling marriages. A parish with the resources to do so could put together its own homegrown support group, customized to the typical needs in the lo-

cal community.

- Mental-health support groups
Whether it is post-abortion healing, fighting the
heroin epidemic, battling depression, grieving
after a loved one's suicide, overcoming addiction
to pornography, or coping with same-sex attraction or gender dysphoria, Catholics and would-
be Catholics struggle just as much as anyone
else does and can benefit from mental-health
support groups.

- Respite care
Caregiving is exhausting, whether it's taking
care of an elder with dementia, a child with special needs, or just being the sole caregiver as a
single parent. When a couple lacks family support or adequate financial resources, even the
"ideal" married couple can be exhausted by the
work of caring for many young children. One of
the challenges of caring for the medically fragile
is that respite caregivers need a level of training
that the average nursery volunteer might not be
ready to provide, and the family may have difficulty with transportation to drop-off programs.
Respite work is a true one-soul-at-a-time ministry.

- After-school tutoring
At this writing, more than half of American
children do not grow up in a home with their
married, biological parents. The picture is even
bleaker when education and poverty levels are

taken into account. Put succinctly: The children who could most benefit from extra academic support are those whose families would most benefit from extra spiritual and social support. Parents who need the most help from the church are those who also are likely to struggle with finding and paying for after-school care.

It takes less than a minute to write out a list of the spiritual works of mercy. Carrying them out is a grueling slog. As Catholics, we need to overcome the divide between the parish insiders who have it all together and those other sinners over there whose messy, complicated, unfixable lives are the ones Jesus wants us to share.

Events That Answer Spiritual Questions

At present, typical converts to the Catholic Church fall into one of two camps: people who did their own study and decided to become Catholic, and those who encountered Jesus in the Mass one way or another and decided to stick around. Much of the Church is operating on DIY evangelization. It is no wonder that the number of "Nones" continues to grow every year.

Evangelization is the opposite of an all-or-nothing proposition. We go out to the world and invite everyone to come in. When we invite them to come and see, we must have landing places where the curious and the seekers can get answers to their questions before they are ready to be Catholic.

- Catholic Q&A sessions
  A sign for RCIA at a parish in my area asked, in giant print, of all driving by on the highway in front of the Church, "What Do Catholics Really Believe???" It's a question many need answered before they begin RCIA, or need answered at

times other than the annual RCIA inquiry period. Periodic no-commitment Q&A sessions can
be built around a theme or just take all comers.
These can be hosted at the parish, on the street,
in a reserved room at the public library, or at a
nearby watering hole.

- Beginner Bible studies
  Catholic Bible studies tend to be scattershot and
  insider focused. Catholic Christian Outreach
  (cco.ca) offers a series of faith studies, beginning
  with the Discovery book, designed to introduce
  participants to the very basic Gospel message.
  Other possibilities for community-friendly, entry-level Bible studies are seasonal 101s, such as
  studying the nativity stories around Christmas-
  time.

- Parenting classes
  Children don't come with an instruction man-
  ual. Whether it's figuring out how to cope with
  the demands of a newborn or how to navigate
  the trials of the teenage years, parents can use
  encouraging, practical support. One of the challenges is distinguishing between classes for disciples and the needs of those who do not yet hold
  to the Faith. Our mission must be faithful to the
  truth on hot-button topics, such as chastity, but
  when presenting to an audience of nondisciples,
  we must acknowledge and plan for the fact that
  the audience does not yet accept Catholic teaching in those areas.

- Vacation Bible school
  Adults have spiritual questions, and so do kids!
  Like those for adults, outreach programs for
  children should begin with the basic Gospel
  message. Catholic how-tos and moral rules and
  regulations come only after our friends have
  made the decision to become disciples.

In creating spiritual landing places for non-Catholics and bare-ly-Catholics, it's important that we set aside a false sense of so-called egalitarianism. One of the tendencies among Catholic faith-formation leaders is to feel that it is somehow shameful or embarrassing to be a person who does not yet accept or understand the Catholic Faith. According to this warped way of thinking, all ignorance is culpable ignorance.

Few of us would admit to such a belief, but our actions betray it. With a humility free of all condemnation, we must be able to say frankly, "This class is a basic introduction to the Gospel message," or "That class is better suited to those who have been practicing the Faith for some time and have already completed a program of study equivalent to x, y, and z." As a presenter with Family Honor (a Catholic chastity-education apostolate that gives workshops for parents and teens), I would love for host parishes simply to let people know, "The assumptions with these programs is that you are desiring to follow Catholic beliefs about human sexuality, and you are seeking to be equipped with the tools to do so."

Taking a one-soul-at-a-time approach can simplify this. Aggressively promoted classes and workshops should be geared toward the nonbeliever (including the nonbelievers in the pews and on the parish council). In one-on-one conversations, disciples from the parish can listen to visitors and fellow parishioners and invite them to more intense study when they are ready for it.

Events for Praying Together

We love God with heart, soul, mind, and strength. If the world cannot find an outlet for their souls in the Catholic Church, where exactly should they go? And yet, as we have seen, the Mass is not meant to be our primary evangelizing event. What are some other ways non-Catholics and barely-Catholics can worship God in our parishes?

- Holiday celebrations
  Twice a year, message boards and parish staff meetings light up with the problem of what to do with the massive influx of visitors who attend Mass for Christmas and Easter — including many who commit sacrilege with the Sacred Host. One option is heavily to promote pageants, caroling services, candlelight prayer services, and other non-Mass observances of the feast day, scheduled at convenient times, organized in a family-friendly format, and with content suited to visitors who want to "go to church" twice a year, but are indifferent to the Mass.

- Distribution of ashes
  Anyone at all is free to receive ashes on Ash Wednesday. Many priests, especially in convenient locations that draw many annual visitors, choose to hold services for the distribution of ashes (the services that get the most non-Catholic traffic) that are not Masses. Though this is one time a year when a welcoming meal or snack is not appropriate, visitors could be invited to meet with parishioners who are available to listen to and pray for specific prayer requests.

- Sing-alongs
  One of the great comic tragedies of Catholic life is the desperate attempt of music directors to satisfy hundreds of parishioners with just four carefully chosen hymns a week. Many favorite Catholic devotional songs were never even meant to be sung at Mass, and many enthusiastic and musically talented parishioners are not in a position to perform every Sunday morning anyhow. Regular events in which parishioners and visitors can relax and enjoy singing along to their favorite spiritual music — including rightfully inspiring secular songs — can go a long way toward answering a true need of the soul, and toward easing tensions in the Liturgy Wars.

- Liturgy of the Hours
  Though priests and religious are obligated to pray the Divine Office, it is truly the prayer of the whole church, and anyone is free to pray it. The opportunity for non-Catholics to come and pray the Liturgy of the Hours, especially Vespers, with the congregation is a way to enter deeply into the Catholic spiritual life and to form their souls in accordance with the mind and spirit of the Church.

As we brainstorm ways to add prayer to parish life, a nagging question may come to the fore: Why aren't opportunities for communal prayer throughout the week and throughout the liturgical year already in place? A new pastor may wonder, for example, why he has to reorganize parish office hours or Mass times in order to make it possible for his staff to attend daily Mass?

The answer gets to the reason for this book: In an unevange-lized parish, prayer has not yet become the center of the Christian life.

It is possible that prayer is not the norm yet due to logistical challenges, so reach out to others in your parish and find out if what is blocking their participation in communal prayer is an obstacle such as scheduling, transportation, work, or family obligations. But often the lack of a parish prayer life is a sign that the members of the parish are in need of evangelization. Once we become people who pray, inviting others to come and pray with us will be as natural as eating dinner.

Outward Versus Inward Focus

Turning typical parish events into evangelizing events requires a change of focus. As a parish, we must decide that the purpose of our work is to invite others into the Church and to accompany them on a long, inefficient journey toward a deep, lasting relationship with Jesus Christ in the Catholic Faith. In other words, I am not just hoping that the families who come to the parish festival have a nice experience or leave with good memories, though, of course, I do hope that. I am also hoping that visitors will make a friendly personal connection that is the beginning of something much bigger.

My hopes will, in turn, fuel specific plans for how to conduct my event. I'll ask myself:

- What are ways that newcomers can have time to start a friendship with a member of my parish?
- How can I invite visitors to follow up with another event at the parish that meets a different, perhaps deeper need?
- In what ways can I offer a spiritual encounter, at the level my visitor needs, even if my event is

not, strictly speaking, a spiritual event?

In my plans, I can't treat my visitors as a generic lump of non-Catholic clay. I need to visualize specific situations that will help me better think about deeper spiritual needs. Imagine:

- A pair of teenagers wandering around, one of whom is dealing with depression and the other who is being pressured into sex by her boyfriend.
- A single mom who is exhausted and at her wits' end with her darling but exasperating eleven-year-old, who has gotten into trouble at school for the third time this week.
- A former Catholic who left the Church after being abused by a cleric and doesn't know how to talk about it with his wife, who is "spiritual but not religious" and has been suggesting they visit churches lately.

I put in my mind a variety of very specific visitors, not because those exact people will come, but because I need a clear idea of the different kinds of challenges my visitors are facing and therefore the different kinds of help I might be able to provide.

In some sense, our job is to read and respond to invisible signs that our new friends are carrying around. Imagine for a moment that as you walk down the street, every person you pass has a big sign explaining his or her most pressing problem and the kind of help he or she needs. Instead of seeing the externals of a young woman walking out of the office building, someone you'd normally describe as an attractive young professional with a trendy suit and amazing heels, what if you saw a sign that said, "I wish I were good enough, and I wish I could meet someone who cared about me, not how pretty I am"?

If you saw that sign, you would want to help. You would feel that here is someone who is looking for what you have found in the Catholic Faith. Because she was carrying the sign that so clearly told you what she longed for, you could easily help. You might go up and speak to her and say, "I want you to know that God loves you just how you are. And I'd like to invite you to come hang out with a group of young professionals who meet at the bar by your office once a week, because they are a neat bunch who are looking to figure out the important things in life, and not just live for the latest trend or the next promotion. When I'm with that group, I feel that I can be myself, and people are interested in who I am, not just what I do or how I look."

Unfortunately, people don't walk around with signs telling us their deepest needs. We have to get to know people slowly, building friendships and listening to learn more about them. But I can use the tool of those imaginary signs to say: Okay, if a girl who is really looking for that sense of being loved and valued, and who is looking to meet new friends who love and respect her for who she is, comes to the parish festival, what could I have at the festival that would help her?

How about some free magnets that have an inspirational reminder of God's love? How about a craft table where participants can make their own canvases with such a message, or buy one for the food-pantry fundraiser? How about a bulletin board where people can post prayer requests? How about a table where people can sit down and ask for prayer? How about a mobile confessional that's also a general talk-to-Father station? How about a list of upcoming events with that group of young professionals? How about a welcome station where kind, friendly people sit and listen to you chat over lemonade?

Instead of viewing the parish festival as food, drinks, and games for the entertainment of parish families, I've started thinking of it as a mission field. I don't want to waste a single opportunity to help someone find what he or she really comes looking for when he or she wanders into my parish event.

> *"Now those who take a superficial and unreflecting view of things observe the outward appearance of anything they meet, e.g., of a man, and then trouble themselves no more about him. The view they have taken of the bulk of his body is enough to make them think that they know all about him. But the penetrating and scientific mind ... inquires into the qualities of the man's soul."*
>
> — Saint Gregory of Nyssa, On Virginity

The Acceptability of the Christian Message

If there is one thing that has been hammered into many of us in the Western world, it's that talking about Jesus is a big, fat no-no. We don't want to offend. As one of my older relatives would say, never talk about religion, politics, or money, and you can get along with anyone.

This is one reason why parish missionary initiatives are so important: If people come to the Catholic Church, they have a reasonable expectation that we will talk about the Catholic Faith.

There are some famous counterexamples of this that have made the news. We can think of situations where a Catholic school had become well established as one of the cheaper options among the local prep schools, and in the effort to keep tuition money rolling in, the school had watered down the Gospel to satisfy non-Catholic or barely-Catholic families, often for generations. After enough years of not teaching the fullness of the Faith, it is unsurprising when parents or teachers rebel against a bishop or principal who insists on Catholic teaching in a controversial area.

That is not the situation we are talking about. In your missionary efforts, you are not going to put out a table at the parish festival that is nothing but literature about divisive, hot-button topics. (You probably do want one or two calm, charitable go-to parish missionaries who can step in and chat if someone shows up and tries to pick a fight about Catholic doctrine.)

No one is shocked, however, to learn that Catholics believe in God. No sane person will be alarmed if a Catholic event opens with prayer. Though we must be careful to avoid proselytizing by making the receipt of support services dependent on lip service to the Gospel, it is normal for someone who wants to talk about spiritual matters to go to a church for that purpose. Where else would someone go to talk about God?

The key is to remember that our chief approach is to pose open-ended questions and then listen intently. Through our commitment to listening first and talking second, we can avoid giving offense, because our answers will focus on the needs that our new friend has expressed.

No Money? No Volunteers? Start Smaller

I have laid out some grand ambitions for parish events. Our Lord summed up the problem succinctly: "The harvest is plentiful, but the laborers are few" (Mt 9:37). Your parish may be struggling to keep the lights on and the roof intact. I can say for myself that at the time I wrote this chapter, my parish Bible study was almost completely unpromoted, not because I didn't want to reach out to newcomers, but because I was working seventy-hour weeks, and the choice was either to cancel the Bible study altogether or just skate by on the bare minimum of evangelistic effort until my work schedule lightened up.

Real life happens. Pastors must pick and choose their priorities. At our parish, Father's number-one goal on his arrival some years ago was a weekly men's prayer group, open to all comers and meeting before the workday begins. Why start there? Because he has to pray the Divine Office anyway, and building up the men of the parish in their spiritual lives would be foundational to all future initiatives. (Lest you worry about sexism here, know that when the parochial vicar arrived, his first major long-term initiative was getting the women's Bible study up and running.)

At a ministry level, leaders must pick and choose their highest priorities. Would the women of my Bible study like to do more work with the homeless? Yes, we would. Is that an option right now? No, it isn't, because all of our members are currently engaged in other, equally necessary work as our vocations call us elsewhere. For the moment, we settle for praying each week for the homeless in our community, by name when possible, and when the time comes to start a second initiative, we'll know.

Events Are Only a Beginning

Whether it be showers for the homeless or sports for the restless, our outreach activities are not evangelization if there is no long-term plan for continued spiritual relationships. Events are bridge builders. They allow those who are willing to take the walk across the chasm to meet welcoming, loving Catholics. In the chapters ahead, we'll see how that initial introduction to Catholicism can lead to growth and transformation, step by step, into full-fledged discipleship.

For Reflection

- What events does your parish or ministry currently host? To what extent are those events drawing others into the Church?
- How can you change existing events to make them more powerfully evangelizing? What are some ways you can add opportunities for forming relationships? What are

some ways you can add opportunities for follow-up?

- In your community, what opportunities do you have, either by going out into the streets or by inviting outsiders in, for reaching those who have no relationship with the Catholic Faith?

- Of all the possible ideas you have for outreach and evangelization, where do you think your energy is best spent right now?

Saints for Evangelists

Blessed Victoire Rasoamanarivo (August 21)

Madagascar native Victoire Rasoamanarivo (1848–1894) could be considered a patron of the role of the laity in parish life. She attended Catholic school as a teenager and chose to be baptized in 1863. Her parents threatened to disown her if she continued to follow the Catholic Faith, but she held firm. She wanted to pursue religious life, but she accepted her parents' plans for an arranged marriage to a cousin instead. Her husband was violent and unfaithful, and she prayed intensely for his conversion. Her willingness to set aside her fears and face down any difficulty would soon become essential to the survival of the Catholic Church in Madagascar.

In 1883, Catholicism was outlawed. Victoire and other Catholics ignored the laws and continued to practice the Faith. Victoire became a leader in resisting government persecution and in working to keep Catholic schools open, even shaming police guards into letting Catholics into their boarded-up churches. For three years, all priests were banned from the country; when they returned in 1886, they found that the Faith had been kept alive and was thriving, thanks to evangelical work of laymen and laywomen like Blessed Victoire.

On his deathbed in 1888, her husband asked for forgiveness and to be baptized. Victoire spent the remainder of her life in prayer and in service to prisoners, the sick, and the poor.

17

Retreats

Countless lives have been changed in just hours by the chance to meet Jesus Christ through a retreat, a Bible study, or another church-sponsored program. What makes an event work well? What are realistic expectations? Why does a program that worked so well for one person turn out to be an absolute flop for another?

Key Points

- People will usually move up only one spiritual threshold, at most, on a given retreat experience.
- Follow-up is needed if the participant is to keep on growing.
- Don't expect a single guest speaker or special event to transform your parish.
- One-size-fits-all retreats and Bible studies are unrealistic and undesirable. One-size-fits-all thinking slowly whittles down a parish to people of that one spiritual size.

The opportunity to get away, reflect, pray, and spend time in a nurturing and inspiring environment allows for healing, insight, and renewal. Some better-known programs include Alpha, Christlife, Cursillo, Steubenville conferences, and Casting Nets ministry training, and there are many excellent video courses offered by reputable Catholic publishers. Most dioceses and many parishes offer tailor-made events.

None of these will solve all your parish problems and convert the world in six convenient forty-five-minute sessions. Any reputable retreat, conference, parish, or home-based study, however, can be a helpful tool for evangelization when used in the right context.

Choosing the Right Retreat or Study

Every retreat or Bible study is designed for a particular range of spiritual readiness. When we match up the right person with the right retreat, great spiritual progress can be made in a short time. The timelessness of the Gospel and the all-powerful grace of Our Lord give retreat leaders a little cushion in preparing their messages, but still we must firmly resist the idea that "Just come to the retreat!" is a cure-all for those we wish to evangelize. We need to consider carefully whom a given retreat is designed to serve.

For someone at the stages of *trust* or *curiosity*, a suitable retreat or study will focus on God's love and healing, while discussing the Faith in clear, understandable ways that avoid assuming any level of background knowledge. Even when someone has an extensive background in Catholic education and therefore knows all the vocabulary and all the moves of Catholic worship, a deeper heart-and-soul understanding of the Faith is still lacking if the person is at the trust or curiosity stage.

At these stages, the participant is not ready for the demands of discipleship. The goal should be to inspire an openness to seeking the Lord. That means that the focus may need to be on overcoming fears, concerns, or misunderstandings about the Faith. The retreat or study will include a clear proclamation of the Gospel, expressed in a way that speaks to the questions the participants bring with them to the event.

For someone who is at the stage of *openness*, the question that the retreat or study must answer is this: Is God calling me? Is there something more? Can I be part of that something more? The individual needs to hear that God is inviting not just people in general but him or her, specifically, despite the person's past and despite his or her brokenness. The retreat or study should show a way to God that is both Catholic and accessible to the one attending. Through the activities of the event, the participant should see that Catholicism isn't just for people who are this age, or this marital status, or this level of education, or this culture, but that Catholicism is also for the individual, the one who has until now felt like the odd man out.

The retreat or Bible study needs to give a concrete invitation: If you would like to learn more, here is a specific next step. If you feel God is calling you, here is a specific way you can answer that call.

For someone who is at the stage of *seeking*, an appropriate retreat or study includes an invitation to discipleship. The assumption is not that the participant is already a disciple. Thus, a focus on a rigorous spirituality with intense self-examination isn't a fit. Let's look at how Jesus called Peter, as found in Luke 5:1–11.

Peter and his brothers had been looking for the Messiah. Then Jesus brought his teaching to Peter. His invitation came first in a request for help. "While the people pressed upon him to hear the word of God, he was standing by the lake of Gennesaret. And he saw two boats by the lake; but the fishermen had gone out of them and were washing their nets. Getting into one of the boats, which was Simon's, he asked him to put out a little from the land. And he sat down and taught the people from the boat."

The next thing Jesus did was to show Peter that he is Lord. "And when he had ceased speaking, he said to Simon, 'Put out into the deep and let down your nets for a catch.' And Simon answered, 'Master, we toiled all night and took nothing! But at your word I will let down the nets.' And when they had done this, they enclosed a great shoal of fish; and as their nets were breaking, they beckoned to their partners in the other boat to come and help them. And they came and filled both the boats, so that they began to sink."

A retreat or study geared toward the seeker must answer the question: Is Jesus Lord? Is Catholicism true? Is all this Christian stuff real? Is it worth giving my life to?

Note that at this point Jesus hadn't asked Peter to make a commitment. He hadn't given Peter a to-do list or a recipe for holiness. Our Lord has only shown Peter that he is God.

"But when Simon Peter saw it, he fell down at Jesus' knees, saying, 'Depart from me, for I am a sinful man, O Lord.' " It was Peter who recognized his unworthiness before God. A retreat or study geared toward the seeker is focused primarily on the holiness and power of God, not on the unholiness and powerlessness of men.

"For he was astonished, and all that were with him, at the catch of fish which they had taken; and so also were James and John, sons of Zebedee, who were partners with Simon. And Jesus said to Simon, 'Do not be afraid; henceforth you will be catching men.' And when they had brought their boats to land, they left everything and followed him."

It was after Peter expressed his faith that Jesus extended the invitation to follow him. A well-designed retreat will not assume that all participants are ready to become disciples. There will be an opportunity for participants to hear the call, and an invitation to come follow the Lord if they are ready to do so.

After reaching the threshold of *discipleship*, the needs are different. A disciple has made the decision to drop the nets and follow Jesus. Though all of us are living lives of constant conversion, there is a difference between the repentance of a disciple and the repentance of a seeker. For the seeker, the primary spiritual task at hand is to understand that God loves, God saves, and God invites. Out of ignorance or inexperience, the seeker's initial conversion is unlikely to involve a clear understanding of his or her culpability for specific sins.

Self-examination is a skill that grows over time, and developing that skill can be a legitimate task at a retreat or study for disciples. For a disciple, the process of ongoing conversion involves acknowledging and repenting of persistent or newly recognized sins. This requires a combination of re-preaching Christ's mercy — lest we despair in the face of habitual sin — and sound catechesis to help the participant more clearly form his or her conscience. Disciples, however, vary in their readiness for rigorous spiritual discipline. Saint Paul writes to the church in Corinth: "But I, brethren, could not address you as spiritual men, but as men of the flesh, as infants in Christ. I fed you with milk, not solid food; for you were not ready for it; and even yet you are not ready" (1 Cor 3:1–2). Just as a man fathers his children differently, depending on their age and maturity, so retreats and studies for disciples will differ depending on the spiritual maturity of the participants.

> *"Be confident that you will accomplish this by simplicity of sound doctrine and by the word of God which penetrates more than any two-edged sword. You will easily be able to contain the attack of enemies and blunt their weapons when in all your sermons you preach and present Jesus Christ crucified."*
> —Pope Clement XIV, *Cum Summi*, "Proclaiming a Universal Jubilee," 1769

Realistic Retreat Expectations

There are certain well-established retreats that have a solid reputation. Year after year, participants consistently report that their relationship with God has been forever changed by attending one of these time-tested retreats. Here are some realistic expectations to help you understand how such retreats fit into the bigger picture of evangelization.

The retreat has well-defined, carefully developed methods and goals. Successful evangelizing retreats are honed over years of trial and error. The retreat will plainly state its target audience and its purpose, and retreat activities will be designed to achieve the stated retreat goals.

Follow-up spiritual support is built into the event. This may consist of the regular weekly or monthly meetings of the association that is hosting the event, or it may be that a local parish Bible study or other group serves as the "ordinary time" home for retreatants. Either way, retreats with long-standing impact are those in which participants continue to build on what they received from the retreat via ongoing prayer, fellowship, mentoring, and study as a part of their regular lives as Catholics.

No one goes from zero to canonized in a weekend. A realistic expectation is that a major retreat experience will move the participant one step further in the five thresholds of discipleship. What this means is that if you invite someone who is at the trust or curiosity stage, and that person has a truly deep and meaningful encounter with God at the retreat, it is highly unlikely that that person has moved all the way into full-fledged discipleship.

Conversion Takes Time

Now, if you are Saul of Tarsus, a Scripture expert who is physically knocked down and blinded by God, and God then speaks out loud to you, and then you follow orders to go to the nearby city, and you fast for three days, and then someone God has ordered to speak to you shows up and heals you … then maybe your retreat experience will involve covering lots of steps in a short time.

Most of us, which is to say basically everyone in our parishes, at any time, are not going to have this experience. We come to know God slowly over time, taking two steps forward, one step back, three sideways, and four on our knees, as bit by bit we inch our way toward intimacy with God. That doesn't mean there aren't times of intense spiritual growth. But growth is the perfect metaphor.

Like a growing child, we consume voraciously right before we have a big growth spurt. That spurt is at most a very small percentage of our total long-term growth. And then after a big spurt, we spend time filling out our present stage of development before we start hungering after the food that we need to fuel our next big step.

Implications for Parish Life

It is easy to mistake the intellectual and social enthusiasm of the *trust* and *curiosity* thresholds for committed discipleship. In an environment like the Catholic Church, where cultural heritage and family custom play a large part in the life of faith, many who attend Mass every Sunday and are actively involved in parish life do not have a profound relationship with Jesus Christ. They are good, loving people who find great comfort in their faith, but their faith is not yet fully grown. Whose is?

We shouldn't view this as a failure. All Catholics this side of the grave are living somewhere short of perfect union with God. When our own faith is weak, the strength of our community can help us along. All of us go through life being both the paralytic carried to Jesus by friends who pick us up when we can't go on alone and the friends who do the carrying.

What we need to do, then, is be grateful that our Church is

one that has a place for pilgrims at all steps on the journey. It isn't fair to assume that Jane Helpful, who is so wonderful about making parish funeral meals, is a disciple. Maybe she is; maybe she isn't. We have to listen and find out. There is no question that she can cook. There is no question that she loves God and loves neighbor. But spiritually, where is she?

If Jane is still at the very early stages of her relationship with God, then it would be cruel to expect her to take on ministry responsibilities that require a mature, adversity-tested, prayer-fueled level of discipleship. When Jane comes back from the Cooking with Jesus Ministry Retreat and is on fire and excited about all she experienced, that doesn't mean she drank a liter of Saint John of the Cross Instant Holiness Powder Beverage Mix and now we can throw any spiritual demand her way.

It means she probably has made a big step from *trust* or *curiosity* to perhaps as far as *openness*. Our next step isn't to throw her into shark-infested waters and see how she swims. Our next step is to help her grow at the *openness* level. A long-term commitment to prayer and study and listening with Jane can prepare her to take the leap into *seeking* when the time comes.

In contrast, in listening we might find out something completely different. Perhaps quiet, humble Jane, who never says much and hates to talk about herself, is, in fact, a disciple of the most profound and unshakable level. Perhaps we have been overlooking the perfect spiritual companion to come alongside and gently and patiently evangelize another parishioner through one-on-one mentoring.

The key here is that we don't make assumptions. We don't let enthusiasm or a recent experience or lots of Catholic-brand chit-chat confuse us. In a parish where very few are disciples, it is easy to mistake *curiosity* or *openness* for *discipleship* because a recent arrival at that stage stands out so boldly against a sea of people going through the motions at a very low level of *trust*.

As on any trek, in order to be an effective guide, we must know not just where we are going but also where we are right now.

For Reflection

- Has a retreat or Bible study made a difference in your life? What was it like? Where were you, spiritually, beforehand? In what way did that retreat or study change you?
- Think about a retreat or study currently offered at your parish or by your ministry. Where along the thresholds of conversion would this study be most helpful? Who would find this event overwhelming or confusing? Who would find this event boring or lacking substance?
- If you were to design the perfect retreat or study for yourself right now, what would you want it to include? What kinds of prayer? What kinds of companionship? What kinds of quiet time or activities?

Saints for Evangelists

Blessed Francisca de Paula de Jesus (June 14)

Blessed Francisca de Paula de Jesus (1810–1895), affectionately nicknamed Nhá Chica by her fellow Brazilians, was a freed slave whose life's mission was to care for the poor and to offer spiritual consolation to all who came to her. She and her older brother were orphaned as children and had to beg in the streets for their food. She decided not to marry in order to devote herself to a life of prayer and service to the poor; though she had virtually nothing herself, she shared her excess with any who asked. Her two-room hovel became a sanctuary for anyone who needed refuge, and people of all walks of life came to her for spiritual guidance.

Francisca inherited her brother's estate on his death in 1861 and used the funds to build a chapel in her impoverished neighborhood so that the poor of the city would have a retreat center. It is now the Shrine of the Immaculate Conception in Baependi, Brazil.

18

Proclaiming the Kingdom

Share the Good News! That sounds great, but what is that news? When we proclaim the Kingdom, we explain the basic facts of God's involvement in human history, from the dawn of creation until the end of time. What are some ways to share the Gospel message in order to be understood by the person in front of me right now?

Key Points

- When we proclaim the kingdom, we share the facts of creation, original sin, the Incarnation, the Crucifixion, the Resurrection, and the life of the Church as the kingdom of God here and in eternity.
- By listening to our friends, we can proclaim the kingdom in ways that answer their personal questions about God's role in their lives.
- Sharing your story of how God has acted in your life is a personal, undeniable way of sharing the Good News.

I had the chance to sit down with a couple who wanted to talk to me about their son's education. The parents are first-generation immigrants from a traditionally Buddhist country, and after we talked about academics, the topic moved to discussing the faith taught at their son's private school. The parents had no objection to their son's studying Christianity or becoming a Christian, but the father explained that he and his wife were devoted Buddhists. I asked them to tell me more about what that meant in their lives, and they told me about some of their beliefs and practices.

"It's basically the same as Christianity," he explained to me. "We all believe that if you live a good life, you go to heaven."

Now, remember that as I'm listening, I'm not trying to find out what "official Buddhist teaching" is. I am interested in hearing about my friend's personal relationship with God, whatever that might be.

"It's interesting you should say that," I replied after listening carefully and asking follow-up questions, "because actually that's an important difference. What makes Christianity different from other religions is that we find we can't be good enough. No matter how hard we try, we just aren't able to be as good as we ought to be. Jesus Christ came to die for our sins so that we could be forgiven and go to heaven even though we aren't good enough to get into heaven on our own."

My observation was part of a much longer conversation and was said with no confrontation or argument; I learned much more than I taught. But that single moment when I talked about the Incarnation was an act of proclaiming the kingdom.

Unique Needs, Unchanging Truth

When we proclaim the kingdom of God, we don't stand up and read a canned announcement. The Good News is unchanging, but every human heart has its own struggles. We've talked about what the Gospel is, but let's recap:

- God loves us, and he created us for an eternal relationship with him.
- Because of original sin, our world is fallen and our relationship with God is broken.
- Jesus, who is God, became man to restore that relationship. He suffered, died, was buried, and rose from the dead on the third day. He ascended into heaven and is seated at the right of the Father.
- The Church was created and commissioned by Jesus to be the vehicle of his presence in our fallen world.
- The sacraments are the ordinary means of entering into a saving relationship with Jesus Christ.

There are many details to fill into that bare outline. Depending on the types of struggles, questions, and background experiences our friends have, we are going to focus our proclamation of the kingdom on different parts of those details.

> *"And there is none other name of the Lord given under heaven whereby men are saved, save that of God, which is Jesus Christ the Son of God. ... This, beloved, is the preaching of the truth, and this is the manner of our redemption, and this is the way of life, which the prophets proclaimed, and Christ established, and the apostles delivered, and the Church in all the world hands on to her children."*
> —Saint Irenaeus, The Demonstration of the Apostolic Preaching

Listening, Listening, Listening

What are some examples of that differing focus?

If my friend is struggling with the problem of evil, then, in proclaiming the Good News, I want to talk about Christ suffering with us. We might want to look at Psalm 22, which Our Lord prayed from Cross, and how God enters into the depth of our suffering and brings us hope. We might want to talk about Christ's agony, the rejection he experienced, and his mission of mercy. All of his miraculous healings were signs of the kingdom precisely because we know that we aren't made for this dark, painful world, and thus, healing the effects of original sin — including illness and death — is a herald of the eternal happiness to come.

If my friend's big question is whether God is even real, I may want to look at evidence for the historical reality of Jesus Christ and of his divinity. I will want to listen and ask many questions to find out where my friend's doubts lie. Is it a question of not "feeling anything" in previous efforts at religious observance? Is it due to being raised in a home where God's supposed nonexistence was simply a fact? Is it due to having never met a Christian who provided a logical, intellectually rigorous discussion of the topic?

If my friend is decidedly Christian but skeptical (at best) of Catholics, then the Church and the sacraments will form a significant part of our conversation. How can Catholic theology be understood in light of a non-Catholic Christian's ways of speaking and thinking about the Faith? Where is the common ground? I will need to listen carefully to make sure I know what my friend really believes, not making assumptions based on denominational background. My message, in proclaiming the kingdom, will be one of finding a deep, intimate encounter with God through the grace of the sacraments.

There isn't a different Gospel for each of these situations. Nor should we imagine that each of these situations is completely different. Someone might be struggling with belief in the existence of God because of struggles with the problem of evil. But we must step outside of our preconceived notion of "what non-Catholics need to know."

For some, Mary and the other saints are a huge stumbling block, but for others, the saints are so intuitively obvious that the communion of saints forms a bridge to belief. Some will have heard the basic Gospel message so many times that they could recite it in their sleep; others will have literally never heard someone explain what the Gospel is at all.

For me as a lapsed Catholic, God's love was never a question. It was something I had absorbed from my earliest days, so deeply built into my being that I couldn't tell you where I got it from. I was in the ironic position of fully believing in the unconditional and absolute love of a God whose historical Incarnation I wasn't quite sure was real. In my conversion, though, it wasn't the historical proof of God that changed my mind, but rather, God's sweeping me off my feet with a spiritual encounter I did not dare resist.

Sharing Your Story

Imagine you are the sentry on the borders of a wondrous country. There was a time when your country was overrun by thieves and rebels, but now the rightful leader has been restored. Even as the enemy continues to resist, the call has been put out by the lawful government: Let all who wish to be citizens of this land come and join us in restoring justice and peace!

You have a neighbor — remember, you live on the border of this country — who doesn't believe that the lawful ruler has taken office. "Tell me about this so-called leader," your neighbor challenges you. "After all, just the other day, rebels were breaking in over at the Jones house. I've seen the rebels, but I've never seen this supposed leader of ours. How can you say the government has been restored?"

It's a fair question, and you want to give it a good answer. You have some choices. You could talk about the facts of the recently won war, or the institutions of the new government, or mention that up in the next town, the courthouse has been rebuilt and cases are being heard.

What else could you do? As it happens, you have personally seen for yourself, and spoken to, the rightful leader of your country. "Let me tell you," you say to your friend, "about how I met our leader." You share the story of what you were doing, and what you saw and heard and felt, and how, ever since that day, your life has been changed. You know where to go and whom to talk to when you have a problem. When you see the rebels out there making trouble, you have hope because you have seen for yourself that your country's soldiers are working to restore order.

Your story has power, because it is true and undeniable.

Proclaiming Your Encounter with the King

As a Christian disciple, you have had an encounter with the King of the universe. Is our world still plagued by the arrows of the enemy? Yes, it is. But you know in your heart that God will prevail and that heaven is real, because you, personally, have felt, or seen, or heard God acting in your life. You remember a time before you knew him as well as you do now. You remember the things God did that opened your eyes and drew you closer to him.

Tell that story. Your story of your relationship with God is your story of the kingdom of God. Someone can argue all afternoon about whether this piece of historical evidence or that bit of philosophical reasoning is valid. Your story of Jesus' acting in your life isn't up for debate. It happened. People can believe it or not, but there's no changing the fact of what God has done for you.

The Facts That Change Hearts

If apologetics is the art of mounting logical proofs, proclaiming the kingdom is something bigger and simpler. At my conversion, in the moment of proclamation, it wasn't a question of "Here is the proof you've been looking for." My colleague simply told me what was. Speaking with the inspiration of his attentive awareness of God's prompting, he declared: This is real. Let me show you. Look through the Bible with me. See what God has to say to you.

In proclaming the kingdom, we are, above all, speaking truth into the lives of our friends. We are stating the plain reality of God's actions in this world. In our daily conversation, we speak the truth over and over again in small things we say:

"There is no sin that cannot be forgiven."

"God loves you so much."

"The Church is always open to you, no matter what."

"Every person is loved by God."

But we also proclaim the big picture at times. We deliver a wide-angle snapshot of the Gospel by sharing the main message of creation, sin, redemption, and eternal life. Though our snapshot will feature in the foreground our friend's most pressing questions, the picture will include the fullness of the truth by telling the whole story of salvation from beginning to end.

For Reflection

- In your own words, what are the basic facts of the Christian faith?

- Are there questions you have about Catholic beliefs concerning creation, sin, Jesus, or salvation? Who can you talk to in order to get good, clear answers to your questions?

- When has someone, in sharing an opinion on God, included ideas that were untrue? How could you take those ideas and respond in a warm, understanding manner by proclaiming the kingdom?

- What is your "God story"? How has God acted in your life? What are the events that led to your giving yourself completely as a disciple of Jesus Christ?

Saints for Evangelists

Blessed Francis Xavier Seelos (October 5)

Blessed Francis Xavier Seelos (1819–1867) was a German seminarian who heard about the plight of German immigrants in the United States and volunteered to become a missionary priest for the Redemptorists. In due time, he was ordained in Baltimore, Maryland, and served in several American cities. Under the tutelage of Saint John Neumann, he became known for his kindness and expertise in spiritual direction and was sought out by Catholics of every ethnicity.

Blessed Francis had a charism for teaching the Faith to Catholics of all ages and states of life, explaining the Scriptures and turning hearts to Christ in the sacraments. After a series of roles of increasing responsibility, he declined the office of bishop and became an itinerant missionary. His final assignment was to a parish in New Orleans, where he died while caring for the sick during an outbreak of yellow fever.

19

The Ask

Your neighbor has been praying for a sign from God — and that sign just might be you. In evangelization, sometimes we have to break down and use our words explicitly to invite someone to follow Jesus Christ. What are some ways this is done? How do we overcome the raw terror that many of us feel when we consider the possibility that we might have to speak up?

Key Points

- Sometimes God will call you to open your mouth and specifically ask another person to accept Jesus Christ in the Catholic Faith.
- There is no one formula for instant converts. Discern what it is that this soul in front of you needs to hear in order to find the courage to follow Jesus Christ.
- A friendship built on unconditional love allows words to be given and received with compassion, mercy, and confidence.

Let me be honest here. I am a shy person. I do not like getting out of my comfort zone, and I definitely do not like making you get out of yours. The uncertainty of explicitly asking someone to follow Jesus is exactly the kind of thing I want to avoid with all my heart. I know I'm not the only one.

And honestly? Most of evangelization is not the moment when you have to come right out and ask someone, "Hey, so, you wanna be Catholic? You wanna give your life to God? You wanna turn everything over to Jesus Christ? How 'bout it?"

Most of evangelization is listening. That's easy for shy people. Most of evangelization is paying attention, being kind, doing good things for people, and answering questions. I've got all that in the bag (more or less).

I can hope that by doing all the other things that evangelists do, maybe my friend will take that final step into discipleship without my having to say a word. Maybe Father's homily at Mass, or the talk at the retreat, or a little moment of quiet time with Scripture — maybe that will be the thing. Maybe all I'll have to say is "Would you like to go to RCIA? There's no commitment," and somehow God will work through those months of study, and come Easter, presto change-o, conversion will have taken place.

After all, isn't converting hearts God's job, not ours?

Yes, but God uses us. Sometimes God will call you to open your mouth and specifically ask another person to accept Jesus Christ in the Catholic Faith.

Oh My Gosh! What Do I Say?

Your friend is not a widget being built at the Catholic-making factory. There is no secret formula for Instant Catholics Now! As a true friend and companion, you must discern what your friend needs you to say.

When my husband, Jon, returned to the Catholic Faith, there were three invitations. I said to him, "Our son needs to get to confession. You want me to take him, or would you like to go?" Jon was confused: Was he, a still-kinda-Protestant lapsed Catholic, even able to go to confession? Well, that wasn't my problem. "Tell Father your situation, and he'll either be able to absolve you or he won't. Either way, he'll be happy to talk to you."

Father was more than happy to talk, and it was Father who extended the second invitation, telling Jon, after a long conversation that gave Father a clear idea of where Jon stood spiritually, that he should seek to grow in his faith through prayer and the graces of the sacraments.

Jon took this conversation to mean that he should attend Mass, pray on his own, and go to confession. But then, a few months later, he said to me, "But I wonder if Father meant I should receive Communion? Can I receive Communion?"

And that is when I put out the third ask. I said to Jon, "I bet if you take Father out to lunch and ask him, he'll help you figure that out."

And sure enough, Father was perfectly happy to invite Jon into full communion with the Church over lunch and a serious spiritual conversation that confirmed that Jon was eligible to receive the Blessed Sacrament.

That was a pretty easy ask. Father did the heavy lifting; all I had to do was encourage my (not-shy) husband to show up and speak to the priest.

Your friend, of course, is in a completely different situation. As you invite, invite, invite, most of the time the invitations you extend will be low-stakes baby steps on the path toward faith. Is there a way I can pray for you today? Do you have any questions for me? Would you be interested in attending this event that is well matched to where you are spiritually?

But sometimes you will need to be vulnerable: Would you like to pray with me? Is there anything keeping you from becoming Catholic right now? Would you like to turn your life over to

God right now?

> *"From this loving knowledge of Christ springs
> the desire to proclaim him, to 'evangelize',
> and to lead others to the 'yes' of faith in Jesus
> Christ."*
>
> — CCC 429

Finding Courage and the Right Words

Some people bowl through life never hesitating, never wishing, never wondering. Actions speak louder than words, and words and actions combined are even better! If that is you, then all you need is permission. So I give it: When you realize someone is ready to take the next step in his or her relationship with God, just ask that person. Pray for wisdom, and then give it a shot.

If you are shy, figuring out the ask might be even easier for you.

Have you ever stood on the sidelines, not sure what to do with yourself? Maybe you were in school and were interested in joining a club or trying out for a sport, but you weren't sure they wanted people like you. Maybe you were looking for a job, but you were afraid to apply because you weren't sure you were qualified. Maybe you wanted to make friends with someone who seemed interesting, but you weren't sure how to open up a conversation.

Now think of a time when someone came right up and invited you. You didn't know how to ask, but your friend or coach or teacher or boss or that total stranger just walked right up to you and said, "Hey, have you ever thought about _____?"

You felt a tremendous relief. Yes! You had been thinking about just that! And now that someone asked you, you found the courage to step up and answer your heart's desire.

As evangelists, what we are listening for is this: What is the question my friend is hoping someone will ask?

My husband, Jon, didn't think he could go to confession, even though I knew he wanted to. He needed someone to invite him. Perhaps your friend is curious about what happens at Mass but is too shy to go alone. Perhaps your friend is interested in signing up for RCIA but thinks it's only for people who definitely want to join the Church. Perhaps your friend wants someone to clear up what all this Jesus stuff is about but isn't quite sure what questions to ask. Perhaps your friend is dying for someone to pray with but is too embarrassed to admit something so "weird." Perhaps your friend has been seeking and seeking and seeking the Lord — as I had been — and longs for someone to step up and say, "Yes! This is real! Yes! You are invited!"

As evangelists, our job is to listen and discern. Our job is to pray that God will help us see how we can help our friends find the answers to their deepest longings. That means that sometimes we will have to say, "It seems to me that maybe you are longing for _____. Can I help you with that right now?"

What if I Come on Too Strong and Turn People Away?

We have different reasons for not making the ask. Before, it might have been ignorance. Perhaps you never realized that one of your jobs as an evangelist was specifically to ask people to take the next step in their faith. Sometimes we worry that we will make fools of ourselves or be rejected by our friends. The solution to that is to continue to grow closer to Jesus in his blessed humility, so that we will be spiritually strengthened against the fear of being found "fools for Christ."

But there is a legitimate, holy fear that we will, in our carelessness, say something that will cause another to be turned off by our strong-arm sales tactics.

The solution is to remember that evangelizing is not proselytizing. There are no strong-arm sales tactics for us. By your commitment to listening and to building a strong relationship founded on true friendship, you will become more and more attuned to your friend's feelings and concerns. By your openness to talking about the Faith, you will have allowed your friend to come forward and ask questions and talk for long hours to you about spiritual things. Over time, you will have periodically extended no-pressure invitations to activities that might or might not be of interest to your friend, but you figured, "Why not ask?" You have built much of your friendship on ordinary daily life — not on religious things at all.

You are a true friend. So when it is time to ask, "Would you like to turn your life over to God right now?," it is a natural part of being a true friend. It doesn't come with strings. There will be no temper tantrum, no hard feelings, no sense that the friendship depends on some imaginary conversion timetable. As a true friend, your love isn't tied to church attendance or sacramental milestones or saying the right formulas.

And so, as a true friend, your questions hold no fear. Your faith is well known, and so is your gentle temperament and your unconditional acceptance of your neighbor — as with the good Samaritan on the road from Jerusalem, everyone is your neighbor.

The privilege of being able to make the ask is really the privilege of being the kind of person who can be trusted to ask. You are a person whose words hold life and grace. And so, when you ask your friend if now is the right time to turn to Jesus Christ in the Catholic Faith, you and your friend both know that the words from your mouth are a sign that the Lord has chosen for this moment to use you as his vessel of mercy, love, and salvation.

For Reflection

- Have you ever asked someone to follow Jesus Christ in the Catholic Faith? Have you ever felt that you should but just didn't know how?

- Who invited you to become a follower of Jesus? How did it all happen? Was there one big "ask"? Were there many small steps? Did you hear God's calling through circumstances? Through a sermon? Through prayer? What would have helped you along your way?
- Do you tend to be too fearful, or not fearful enough?
- How can you work on building strong, attentive friendships so that you will be more confident in your ability to discern what to say and when to say it?
- In your own words, make a short, simple prayer to the Holy Spirit that you can pray when you need guidance before you open your mouth — or courage to open it!

Saints for Evangelists

Saint Andrew Kim Taegon (September 16; All Korean Martyrs, September 20)

We do not know when we shall be led out to death, but we are full of confidence in the mercy of the Lord, and trust that He will give us strength to confess His holy Name up to our last moment.
— Final letter of Saint Andrew Kim Taegon to his bishop

Saint Kim Tae-gon Andrew, or more commonly in English, Saint Andrew Kim Taegon (1821–1846), came from a family of martyrs and is one of some ten thousand Korean Christians put to death during a century of intense persecution. His great-grandfather was arrested and sentenced to death for being Christian (he died before Andrew was born); after Andrew went abroad to seminary, his father back home in Korea was executed in 1839.

Andrew was ordained in China in 1845, the first native-born Korean to become a priest, and slipped back into Korea with his bishop to begin his work of evangelization. He was arrested the following year while attempting to lead missionaries from China into the country. Prior to his execution, he preached the Faith to his captors, to bystanders, and to his fellow prisoners. He is the patron saint of Korea.

20

Companions on a Long Walk

Becoming Catholic isn't always easy. How do we help those who want to become Catholic, but perhaps marriage difficulties or other problems stand in the way? What does good pastoral accompaniment look like?

Key Points

- By recognizing the real suffering that our friends experience, we avoid glibly shoving them off to struggle on their own.
- When we strive together for holiness, we dignify our friends with the reality that they, too, are made for perfect union with Jesus Christ, no matter how difficult the path might be.
- When someone cannot receive the sacraments, practical support plays an important role in relieving heavy spiritual burdens.
- The new believer who cannot receive the sacraments needs to be drawn more deeply into the

life of the Church and given the steady companionship of loving Christian friends.

I was confirmed in the Catholic Faith in my senior year of high
school — even earning the parish Catholic Student of the Year
award from the Knights of Columbus. Within a month of starting college, I had quit going to Mass.

It wasn't intentional. I simply got distracted by other activities. I was frequently out of town on the weekends, and I never got
fully connected with my college Catholic center.

One thing led to another, and my weak faith became no faith.
By the time I was getting married, it seemed hypocritical to try to
arrange a wedding at my home parish when neither my husband
nor I believed the Catholic Faith. That was my walk out of the
Church.

So what happened when I returned?

Fast-forward a few years. I had had a profound conversion
experience, shown up at Mass, and been forever changed. Small
problem: My husband and I were not married in the Catholic
Church. As baptized Catholics, this meant that our marriage was
invalid. What was my new pastor to do with a mess like this?

He got to work straightening me out. In the confessional,
he listened to my sins and absolved me — patiently and gently
working through the confused sense of right and wrong that my
poorly formed conscience brought into the box. Outside the confessional, he tactfully — and privately — answered my questions
and gave me information I needed to start resolving my marital
conundrum. His information was accurate and anticipated many
common concerns. At no point did he make assumptions about
whether I was in a state of grace. What he did was give me the
hope that I could be in a state of grace. He showed me the path
for making that happen, both for the time being (living as brother
and sister was an option) and over the long term (through conval-

idation or radical sanation).

Waiting and Waiting on Jesus

Sometimes the barrier between a new disciple and the sacraments is not easily removed. The most common cause is a parishioner's invalid marriage. One of the most painful cases is when an abused spouse must refrain from seeking an annulment due to fear of deadly revenge if the ex finds out about it. In ministering to immigrants, another common barrier is that baptismal paperwork from the country of origin, or legal difficulties with immigration laws in the host country, put an indefinite hold on verifying that the recipient is eligible for a sacrament. We can imagine other less common scenarios as well.

What can we do to help?

Acknowledge that real suffering is involved.

This is true even in cases where the problem is self-created. A cold, "suck it up, buttercup" attitude does not help. In our acknowledgment of suffering, we need to avoid falling off the Christian path into one of two extremes. One lie says, "This should be easy for you! It's God's will! If you can't do it, it's all your fault!" The other lie says, "You are not able to live up to the calling of holiness. Sanctity is for other people, not you. The bar is simply too high for someone like you. So go ahead and sin." What we seek is the narrow road, the middle road of truth: "Yes, this is very, very hard. It hurts to see you suffer. I know it hurts even more to be the one suffering, even if I myself have never experienced what you are going through. I'm sorry you are in this situation, and I'm going to stick by your side and do everything I can to make it a little less bad."

Do what you can.

If you are charged with giving moral advice, provide accurate counsel that explores all legitimate, morally sound options for dealing with the situation. If there are paperwork problems holding up access to the sacraments, find out if there is anything you can do to assist. Look for ways to shore up your struggling friend on all sides. When someone is dragged down by exhaustion, financial burdens, illness, housing complications, lack of childcare, or a toxic workplace, those weights can put on such a squeeze that spiritual matters feel impossible. Lightening the load in a seemingly unrelated area can create space and energy for dealing with deeper difficulties of the heart and soul.

Go deeper spiritually.

Sometimes the person seeking the sacraments has a faulty and superficial faith. Think, for example, of the divorced and remarried couple who, in their pride and anger, stubbornly refuse to regularize their marriage, even though there is good reason to believe that the earlier attempted marriages were null. Sometimes the individual has a sincere, well-meaning faith but is daunted by the sacrifices that the situation requires. The prospect of separating from a current relationship or of living as brother and sister can feel unthinkably impossible, even if others have charted that path and grown greatly in the graces that flow from their sacrifice. And finally, in some cases, there is a true injustice, and an innocent person is being unfairly persecuted despite a perfect desire to do God's will.

Although each person who longs for the sacraments and cannot access them is in a different situation spiritually, we know that the only recourse for all who suffer is to learn to "hide in his wounds" — to grow closer to our suffering Lord. This must be a true one-soul-at-a time walk together, not a dismissive "If only you were holier, this wouldn't bother you." Our Lord was perfectly holy yet was deeply "bothered" by his Passion. Closeness to God does not cause suffering to go away.

Rather than trying to pick fitfully at a friend's problem that won't seem to budge, spend time together, deepening your walk with Jesus through prayer, studying the Scriptures, and carrying out the works of mercy.

Create a place of shelter in the heart of the Church.

When someone cannot receive holy Communion, the tendency is to think of that person as not quite Catholic. Awkwardly we suggest a few devotions to be prayed in the pews, but we aren't really sure that this person otherwise belongs. This is not the way of Our Lord, and it is not the way of a Church that is mother.

What does a mother do with her fussy baby? She carries him around all day, keeping him close. What does a mother do with a child who is sick? She checks on him more frequently than usual, making sure he receives the care he needs; the sicker he is, the closer she stays.

The parishioner who cannot receive the sacraments is the baby with the deadly illness. Where you go, baby goes: to coffee, to Bible study, to adoration, to the restaurant for a night out, whatever you've got.

Build friendships with other compassionate people.

Those who are struggling with unwanted celibacy can find hope in hearing from a priest or a religious who has accepted a celibate vocation. There are many others to pull into the circle of support as well, some of whom are experiencing unwanted celibacy, others who carry a different cross. Think of the widowed, the bereaved, those who have dealt with serious illness or disability, those who struggle financially, those who have experienced infertility … there are many fellow parishioners who have hearts open to consoling those who face profoundly painful trials, even if those trials are not exactly the same.

Who do you know who can be a companion or mentor to

your struggling friend? Consider both those who share similar backgrounds and those who have strikingly different experiences but delightfully compatible temperaments. Invest the time in making introductions and perhaps facilitating the match through a dinner for three, a coffee date, or other small-format, low-pressure encounters.

Accompaniment Is Discipleship

In the final section of the book, we'll look at *discipleship*. A disciple is a kind of student, but not an ordinary student. When I teach English, my students show up for a few hours a week. They learn from me about literature or writing or grammar, and then they move on to other pursuits. A disciple is a student whose course of study is his or her whole life.

The point of Christian discipleship is for us students of Christ to learn how to live as Christ lives. One of the reasons we struggle with accompanying those who cannot yet receive the sacraments is that we lack the art of discipleship. We've broken down the Faith into a single course, about one hour a week — and heaven help Father if he goes five minutes longer — that consists of Sunday Mass attendance.

An hour a week on Sunday is not the entirety of the Catholic Faith. Is it the highlight of our week? Yes. Is it so essential to our spiritual well-being that choosing to miss Mass is like choosing to starve yourself? Yes. Is it right that someone who cannot receive holy Communion should feel a keen absence — a hole in the heart that longs to receive Jesus Christ? Yes indeed.

But that hole in the heart is bleaker and darker when we also deprive our friend of the entire rest of the Christian life. Our mission toward all new Christians, regardless of whether they are able to receive the sacraments, is to train them up in the entirety of the Catholic Faith.

That means living the Christian life together, so that we can learn from each other how to become little Christs in everything we do, not just sitting in the pews an hour a week on Sundays. That's discipleship, and that's what we'll be talking about in the remainder of this book.

> **"Faith and conversion arise from the 'heart,' that is, they arise from the depth of the human person and they involve all that he is. By meeting Jesus Christ and by adhering to him the human being sees all of his deepest aspirations completely fulfilled. He finds what he had always been seeking and he finds it superabundantly."**
>
> General Directory for Catechesis, 55

For Reflection

- Was there a time when you were waiting to receive a sacrament? What was that time like? What did you feel? What helped you during that time of waiting?
- As you think about your gifts and talents, what are some ways you could provide spiritual or practical help to someone in a difficult pastoral situation?
- Make a list of all the ways someone could become immersed in the life of your parish outside of Mass. What are obstacles to involvement, such as lack of childcare or eldercare, that your parish needs to consider in opening the doors to those on the margins of parish life?
- Where in your day-to day-to life could you invite a lonely fellow parishioner to live with you for a few hours? This could be a dinner invitation, a sporting event, a service activity, or anything at all that would give your friend quality time in the company of another believer.

Saints for Evangelists

Blessed Franz Jägerstätter (May 21)

Blessed Franz Jägerstätter (1907–1943) was ultimately martyred for his faith, but not before a long period of wrestling with his conscience and seeking any possible way to avoid the inevitable cost of following Christ. Prior to his marriage, his life was far from pious, but inspired by his wife's deep faith, Franz began studying the Bible and the lives of saints.

When the Germans invaded Austria, he was the only man in his village to vote against the Anschluss; in the years that followed, he worked every legal exemption to evade direct service in the Nazi army. When he was called to active duty in 1943, he declared himself a conscientious objector and offered to be an ambulance driver instead; the offer was ignored, and he was arrested. Friends, including a priest, begged him to save himself by taking the Hitler oath and serving in the army, but he took inspiration from the example of a Catholic priest who had recently been martyred for refusing to serve the Nazis, and he determined to do the same. He was executed in prison in 1943.

Part 3

Discipleship

After you become Catholic, then what? Our final unit looks at *discipleship*, a word that is commonly applied three ways: the act of following Jesus Christ; our experience of learning from our fellow Christians how to live the Christian life; and the work we do in mentoring other disciples.

The Care and Commissioning of Christian Disciples (chapter 21) is a brief explanation of why the learning and teaching aspect of discipleship is so vital to the life of the Church.

Next we'll look at the two absolutely essential ways in which disciples teach and guide one another, in **One-on-One Mentoring (chapter 22)** and **Small-Group Discipleship (chapter 23)**.

In **Catechesis (chapter 24),** we'll turn up the scale of our discipleship efforts another notch and also step back into the work of evangelization. Though this chapter contains some practical brainstorming specific to parish faith-formation programs, our foundation will be in cultivating the mindset of an evangelist in order to proclaim the Gospel more effectively in any setting.

Finally, **Forming Disciples for Ministry (chapter 25)** answers two crucial questions: What role should our parish play as a community of disciples, and what's the goal of making disciples anyway?

Once we answer those, we'll be right back to the beginning, with a few concluding words in **Unleashing the Church Militant**.

21

The Care and Commissioning of Christian Disciples

The journey of faith doesn't end with RCIA. We come full circle in our work of evangelization when we help new or never-commissioned Christians become evangelizers themselves.

Key Points

- Disciples need to be fed well, or they won't grow strong in Christ.
- New believers need guidance and support to help them mature in their faith.
- Catholicism is not a self-service religion. As a community, we must help each other become more like Jesus as we live together day in and day out.

Remember our definition of evangelization? We said that evangelization consists of the concrete actions we take to help our friends become followers of Jesus Christ. During his time on earth, Our Lord had disciples, people who followed him around and learned from him. Today his followers must learn from him through the mission of the Church, which is Christ's body on earth. Disciple-ship, then, is the art of being a disciple. Discipleship includes the things we do to help our fellow Christians recognize and carry out their God-given calling to holiness and Christian service, and it likewise refers to our experience of being spiritually mentored by others. Let's talk about that.

My kids and I enjoy going to the National March for Life when we can, and our visit always involves a stop at the expen-sive but delicious cafeteria in the basement of the National Gal-lery of Art. We drive up to the DC area the day before, spend the night with friends who live in the suburbs, and then we all take the Metro into the city in the morning. Kids don't enjoy stand-ing around in the cold, watching political speeches, so we pick a museum to visit while we wait for the march to get underway. After an hour or so of looking around, we head to the cafeteria to grab lunch, since we know that it will be many hours before we see food and comfort again, given the long ride back out to the suburbs at the end of the day.

Children let loose in a cafeteria choose some interesting foods. Without a parent insisting otherwise, I'm fairly certain that some of my children would try to make it through a winter day outdoors on nothing but Jell-O and fruit punch. Pro-parent-ing tip: Inspect all trays before checking out.

The Self-Service Catholic Cafeteria

No sane adult would be surprised to discover that kids become lethargic and cranky if they don't eat well at lunch. We know that children need parents precisely because they don't always know what their real needs are. It is our job to provide a minimum of supervision to ensure that our children get the physical, spiritual, intellectual, and emotional food they need.

New disciples have similar needs. Someone who has just entered into a profound relationship with Jesus Christ in the Catholic Faith is many things: enthusiastic, energetic, eager, excited — not unlike my kids heading out for the March for Life.

Where disciples are few and far between, that enthusiasm is easily mistaken for self-sufficiency. For those of us disciples in the pews, struggling with our own spiritual weariness at times, it may seem preposterous that someone so obviously committed to the Faith and on fire for the Lord might need our help. Parish leadership, meanwhile, simply can't do it all, and frankly, someone who has truly given himself or herself to Jesus is already so much further along on the spiritual path than the average Catholic that we assume our work is done. New disciples are left to wander the spiritual cafeteria, fending for themselves.

Sometimes this works out. Those who naturally enjoy the study of religion can hope to find books or websites to help them learn all about the Catholic Faith. Catholics who have just experienced a profound conversion might land among a superb group of Catholic friends who provide, intentionally or otherwise, mentoring in the Faith. Unfortunately, many are not so lucky.

All the lectures in the world about taking responsibility or "getting past a second-grade faith" don't change the fact that people who are young in the Faith still need good spiritual parenting. They should not be let loose in the cafeteria to fill up their tray with spiritual Jell-O, unaware of the long, hard march that awaits.

Feed Your Sheep!

It is the primary function of the local parish, which is to say all members of the parish working together as the united Body of Christ, to provide solid spiritual sustenance for new disciples. People who are young in the Faith need the consistent, ongoing company of mature Christians who can show them how the

Christian life is lived. They need spiritual friends who will pray with them, answer questions, teach them how to study Sacred Scripture, and prepare them for their future as adults in the Faith, ready to take on their own missions.

So often, as a result, when we attempt to motivate the disciples of our parish to evangelize, the response that comes is "Feed me!"

This can cause some second-guessing. Maybe these are not yet disciples. Maybe I have assumed someone is further along the spiritual thresholds than he or she really is. That can certainly be the case.

But I have repeatedly found, and others report the same experience, that our fellow parishioners who are, in fact, at the spiritual threshold of discipleship, and who do, in fact, wish to become evangelists, are insistent that they need time first to learn the Faith more fully. I have found this with individuals I know well, whose lives as disciples were long proven to me; I have found this with students who began in Bible study as an unknown quantity and whose spiritual maturity was repeatedly confirmed through long months of conversation. And yet they are not ready to evangelize, and they know it.

They beg for time spent in formation, learning to deepen their relationship with Jesus Christ, and they use the time profitably if you offer the resources. They aren't stalling or foot-dragging. They are starving. Whether they've been disciples for months or years or decades, no one has properly equipped them for the march onto the mission field.

In this final section of the book, we'll see how you and I, regardless of our states in life, can help our parish homes become places where disciples are fed and spiritually parented in preparation for our God-given missions as evangelists.

"But a body calls also for a multiplicity of members, which are linked together in such a way as to help one another. And as in the body when one member suffers, all the other members share its pain, and the healthy members come to the assistance of the ailing, so in the Church the individual members do not live for themselves alone, but also help their fellows, and all work in mutual collaboration for the common comfort and for the more perfect building up of the whole Body."
—Pope Pius XII, *Mystici Corporis*, "The Mystical Body of Christ, the Church," 1943

For Reflection

- How did you learn the Catholic Faith?
- Do you have a group of mature Catholic friends who can provide you with feedback and encouragement as you grow in your faith?
- In what areas do you find yourself wishing you had a teacher or a guide? What kinds of spiritual hunger do you experience?

Saints for Evangelists

Blessed Benedict Daswa (February 1)

Blessed Benedict Daswa (1946–1990) was born in South Africa and converted to Catholicism in 1963. He worked as a teacher and a catechist and helped to build the first church in his area. He was known for his devotion to his family as a husband and father and for his intense sense of spiritual fatherhood to the youth in his community. Though actively involved in the communal life in his tribe, and respected by the chief for his counsel, as a Catholic he was insistent on avoiding the use of traditional forms of magic.

In 1990, elders in his village demanded a tax of all residents in order to pay for sangoma, a medium or spiritualist whose services the elders wanted to hire to figure out why the village was being plagued by heavy rains. Benedict refused to pay the tax. In anger at his refusal, his enemies lured him into an ambush by taking advantage of his willingness to help those in need. He was set upon by a mob, who tortured and killed him. His status as a martyr was confirmed, and he was beatified in 2015.

22

One-on-One Mentoring

Nothing can replace the time-intensive, but essential, work of spending time one-on-one, providing support, encouragement, prayer, and accountability for the disciples in your parish.

Key Points

- One-on-one relationships are where the serious work of discipleship takes place.
- One-on-one mentoring is time intensive. You can mentor only one or two people at a time.
- Allow for personality differences. Wait to commit until both of you are confident that you'd like to take on a regular meeting time.
- Take the big-picture view. Time spent with another disciple isn't about raising revenue or attendance numbers; it is about investing in the kingdom of God.

Once a week for a year, my husband met with a friend before work to read the Bible with him. Where was that friend on the spectrum of evangelization? Was he at the curiosity stage, or the seeking stage? We know for a fact that he was at the "I'd like to get up early and buy you breakfast so we can read through the entire Bible" stage. Over the course of this year together, my husband and his friend both grew spiritually. They grew in their knowledge of the Lord and in their awareness of how to apply God's Word to their lives. If our friend was not a disciple at the start of the year, he was a committed and intensively formed disciple by the end.

Some time later, our friend was chosen to sit on a jury for a gruesome murder trial. He ended up taking a leadership role among the jurors in his Bible-Belt town, explaining to the others how the Bible laid out God's plan of mercy and forgiveness; as horrible as the crime had been, our friend felt that the circumstances of the case still indicated that the death penalty should not be imposed. At least two lives were radically changed by that year-long one-on-one Bible study.

Individual Attention Is Time-Intensive

It sounds impressive to say, "I impacted five hundred people this week with the talk I gave!" or "Eighty kids were confirmed in my program this year!" I can attest that many times my life has been changed for the good by a sermon given to a large audience, delivered by someone who has never met me and probably never will. Large-format evangelization and discipleship are not without value.

But one-on-one mentoring is where the serious work happens. In an individual setting, you can discuss hard issues and confidential personal problems. You can work through problems it would not be appropriate to discuss in a group, such as relationship conflicts or potentially gossip-generating parish challenges. You can follow the conversation wherever it needs to go.

If discipleship is the process of teaching someone, "This is how to be a Christian," one-on-one discipleship allows you to teach, "This is how you can be a Christian."

The One-on-One Challenge

In terms of making one-on-one discipleship happen, the two big challenges are time and personalities.

You simply cannot set aside ten or twelve or thirty weekly one-on-one discipleship meetings. If you are a parent, with some creativity in finding ways to spend time together, you can hope to disciple each of your children. (If you have a large family with many children still at home, only one other discipleship relationship is all you should count on forming; the one you take on should be carefully chosen for compatibility with your state in life.) If you are a pastor, a parish staff member, or a ministry leader, you cannot decide to personally father or mother fifty, five hundred, or a thousand people with the same intimacy with which a parent mothers or fathers a handful. What you can do is choose one or a few parishioners to disciple intensively, in the midst of your broader work shepherding your God-given flock.

Because discipleship relationships are so time intensive, you'll want to do some serious thinking and praying before you get started, allowing God to set up his divine appointments for you.

Here is an example of how God dropped a one-on-one discipleship opportunity into my life. When I was a young mother, I used to sit for an hour every week in the lobby of the dance studio while my three daughters took dance lessons. Another mom, who was a more mature Christian than I was, also used to wait there. We would spend that hour talking about the challenges we faced as Christian mothers, and she would encourage me in areas where I was struggling. That kind of ultra-efficient time usage is the only kind of long-term, nonfamily discipleship responsibility that parents of large families should plan to commit to. Your children are your first priority.

For those who have smaller families or no children at home, discipling one or two other Christians is a realistic goal. The nature of those one or two relationships will depend on where you are in your faith. For a new Christian, look for one experienced, mature Christian to take you under his or her wing, and one good solid Christian peer who wants to grow together. Eventually you will reach a middle age when you should be discipling one person who is less experienced than you in the Christian life, but also continuing to be discipled by someone who is more spiritually mature than you. And finally, there may come a point in your life when you are primarily the giver and rarely the recipient in discipleship relationships, though I don't know any mature Christian who doesn't continue to soak up all wisdom on offer.

For those in ministry, your priority may be on fostering one or a few of the disciples immediately in your care. If you have a sound, cordial relationship with someone who reports to you as an employee or a volunteer, discipling that person is the obvious way to help him or her to grow to the point of being able to take on more responsibility. At times, though, it will be more prudent and also more refreshing to mentor someone who is not part of your work. When it comes to guiding someone through thorny problems of conflict within the Church, it is helpful to have a sounding board in a fellow worker in the vineyard who understands keenly the sting of Church politics but is not personally involved in whatever your troubling situation might be.

Finding the Time

The laborers are few, and the work is immense. Pray for wisdom to discern how to carry out this essential work in a way that doesn't sabotage your vocation. Allow God to introduce you to someone, generally of the same gender, whose schedule coincides well with yours. You are looking for an opening when you can both set aside about an hour to meet someplace where you can talk and pray without interruption. An inexpensive restaurant or coffee house that is quiet enough for conversation but busy enough for others to ignore you often works well. Your home, your office, the public library, the walking track, or the side of the field while the kids are at soccer practice can all work, depending on whether you can count on uninterrupted time. One of the beauties of divine matchmaking is seeing how God will set aside one hour when you and your fellow disciple both happen to be in the same place at the same time — even when your days are otherwise entirely separate.

> *"Therefore, it is of the utmost importance that you choose for the office of communicating Christian teaching to the faithful not only men endowed with theological knowledge, but more importantly, men who manifest humility, enthusiasm for sanctifying souls, and charity. The totality of Christian practice does not consist in abundance of words nor in skill of debating nor in the search from praise and glory but in true and voluntary humility."*
> — Pope Clement XIII, *In Dominico Agro*, "On Instruction in the Faith," 1761

Matching Personalities

I have participated in one formal discipleship relationship. A women's Bible study I belonged to had all the members fill out a questionnaire, and then the group leader matched younger women with older women, pairing them up based on their interests, spiritual needs, and even practical questions such as whether childcare or transportation were concerns.

For some of the partners, those match-made relationships

were beneficial but short-lived. For others, the mentoring relationship continued for a long time, evolving as life circumstances dictated. The reality is that sometimes you hit it off with another Christian, and sometimes that spark of spiritual friendship isn't quite there. Even when you love meeting with someone regularly, your life circumstances may eventually make it impossible to continue.

Finding That Mentor or Disciple

If you are at loose ends, either in need of a mentor or available to mentor a newer Christian, keep a prayerfully friendly attitude toward those you meet. Every now and then, you will feel the Lord inspiring you to extend an invitation: "Could I interest you in a cup of tea sometime next week?" or some other relaxed format. You don't need to set an agenda when you extend your invitation, though if you are looking for a mentor, you may want to indicate that by mentioning something along these lines: "I have some questions that I want to run by you," or "I am hoping to get your thoughts on a few things."

If the other person accepts, then see how it goes. Ask a few open questions, listen, and get to know each other. Do you find that you can easily fill an hour talking about spiritual things at a depth that is satisfying? Do you find that at the end of the hour, you have a sense of having grown in your relationship with God or having gotten a better sense of the direction you need to take?

That is the mark of a good discipleship relationship, regardless of whether you are slated to be the spiritually junior, senior, or co-equal partner in your deepening friendship.

If the hour is awkward or boring, the two of you are probably not a good match. Unless you have a formal obligation to do so, simply move on with your life. Thank your friend for the company and avoid making a further commitment. If your friend asks for follow-up support and you feel you are not the best person to provide it, commit to helping your friend meet other people better suited to providing that help.

Should the two of you hit it off, then suggest that you meet again sometime. An obvious format might have presented itself during your conversation — for example if one of you said, "I've been looking for someone to read through the Gospels with me," and the other lit up with joy and replied, "Me too!"

But it is just as likely that you've simply found someone you'd like to talk with another day, but with no particular plan in mind. Float the idea of a second get-together, and if the other person shows interest, then propose a date. Do not be offended if the other person is not able to commit to a second meeting at that time.

If you continue to make and accept invitations, and pray for the Holy Spirit to work in your life, in time you will settle into an ongoing discipleship relationship with someone who is spiritually compatible with you. Your meetings can be very relaxed and informal, or they can be structured study or prayer time together. The point of getting together isn't to accomplish a specific official discipleship agenda. The point is to grow in your practice of the Faith by spending time with another Christian, intentionally choosing to help each other grow closer to God.*

Intentionality in One-on-One Discipleship Strategies

The time-intensive, almost luxurious nature of one-on-one discipleship can feel woefully inefficient. For a parish leader, it can feel as if all your work has been lost if you invest precious, limited time in someone's life, only to have that person turn around and

---

* Who mentors the mentors? Catholic Missionary Disciples (catholicmissionarydisciples.com) provides one-on-one and small-group formation for parish leaders looking to learn the skills of evangelization and discipleship. Participants form a mini community of colleagues who compare notes and share experiences under the guidance of a Catholic evangelist who has years of hands-on experience in the field.

leave the parish.

Discipleship is like nurturing a tree with legs. You fertilize and water and harden off that sapling, pour hours and hours into growing a good, strong tree in your spiritual yard, only to see that tree pick itself up, walk away, and cast shade and bear fruit somewhere else.

Despite the departure of the tree, the time spent in cultivation is not wasted work. Remember that Our Lord invested three years in just twelve men and then proceeded to tell them to get up and go to the ends of the earth. The normal, natural outcome of a discipleship relationship is that the disciple will eventually move on to other work. Because we are not God, we do not control what that other work will be or where it will happen.

Because we live in a fallen world, we know that every person we disciple will eventually die. That may happen sooner rather than later. Because we believe in the communion of saints, we can be certain that even if our disciple should perish, our work has not perished. The whole goal of discipleship is to prepare one another for heaven. Heaven is the land of fully matured Christians.

For Reflection

- Have you ever been in a one-on-one discipleship relationship, in which you intentionally met with another Christian regularly to talk about your Christian walk and to pray together? If so, what was that like? If not, what is the closest thing to that in your experience?
- What are some natural openings in your schedule when you might be able to meet with another member of your parish, either as a disciple or a mentor? What time of day? What location?
- Who is someone in your parish you'd like to learn from? How can you set up a one-time invitation for the two of

you to spend an hour together getting to know each other?

- Is there someone in your parish (or elsewhere in your life) whom the Lord has laid on your heart? Do you need to give that person a call and see about spending some time together?

Saints for Evangelists

Servant of God Emil Kapaun

Servant of God Emil Kapaun (1916–1951) served as a chaplain in the U.S. Army in World War II but distinguished himself by his fearless service in Korea, for which he would be awarded a Medal of Honor. In addition to his tireless ministering to the troops off the battlefield, he would go onto the field under heavy fire to administer last rites, pull wounded soldiers to safety, or improvise shelter in place for those he could not move.

During a battle on November 2, 1950, when outnumbered U.S. soldiers were ordered to retreat as the Chinese closed in, Father Kapaun chose to remain with the wounded soldiers, knowing that capture was inevitable. The remainder of his priesthood would be spent tending the spiritual and physical needs of his fellow prisoners of war. Under torturous conditions, he maintained morale, tended the sick and the wounded, fearlessly asserted the truth in the face of their captors' propaganda, led the prisoners in daily prayer, and risked his life scavenging every possible source of food, water, and clothing for the POWs. On Easter morning 1951, he openly defied the Chinese prison guards and held an Easter sunrise service. Shortly thereafter, he succumbed to starvation and dysentery; on his way to the shack where the prison guards took him to die, he forgave his captors and made his fellow POWs promise to hold on to their faith.

23

Small-Group Discipleship

Small groups are where community growth happens and new missions are born. What do we mean by a small group, and how do we get one going? How do we know if it's doing any good?

Key Points

- A small group consists of three to seven and no more than ten to fifteen members who meet regularly to pray, study the Faith, and talk about their lives as Christians.
- In some situations, strong leadership may be needed to manage challenging personalities in the group.
- An effective discipleship group has a specific purpose. Its goal is to prepare new Christians to answer their calling from God and help mature Christians persist in their spiritual walk as new challenges arise.

When we talk about small groups, we are referring to a particular type of discipleship activity. In a small group, members gather together to pray for one another, to discuss difficulties, and to grow in their knowledge of God.

The intentional focus on learning more about the Faith and living the Faith makes a small discipleship group different from, say, a typically ladies' night out at the bar. (But you can use a ladies'-night-out format to put together an excellent small group!)

Another trait of a small discipleship group is that there should be a sense of community and a deepening of relationships. In contrast, think about a Bible study in which members show up, learn from an instructor, and go home. This is not a small group in the discipleship sense of the term. A small discipleship group, even if it is built around the exact same Bible study curriculum, will take on a distinctive character:

- Members will share what is going on in their lives, ask questions, offer ideas, and thus, get to know each other more deeply.
- Members will commit to praying for one another through the week.
- Even if someone is part of the group for only a short time, he or she will have grown closer to Christ and closer to the other members of the group during that time.

If you are listening and observing carefully, you may notice that some groups are more accurately considered small evangelization groups. The members are not disciples yet; they are still working through earlier stages of the five thresholds. Take a look at chapter 17 on evangelizing retreats to get ideas about how to tune your group to your members' needs. In a small group, you are taking the same principles for retreats suited to the spectrum of spiritual thresholds and applying them on a smaller scale. If you are the leader, you may need to shift the focus of your small group if you realize that the original plans are not suited to the present spiritual needs of your group members. As a participant in a group, your attentiveness to other members can give you insight into how to help steer group discussion when there is a need to do so.

How Small Is Small?

A small group means a gathering of three to seven people. You can go a little larger than that, but not much — fifteen maximum. This size allows everyone time to get to know one another and to be able to share, and it helps prevent quieter members of the group from getting lost on the sidelines.

At the larger end of the spectrum, though, it will take significantly more time to accomplish an equivalent level of relationship building and spiritual sharing, so larger groups are better reserved for situations in which members already know each other well from other contexts and are in very similar states of life, or in family-to-family or couple-to-couple groups.

Sometimes there is crossover between larger parish groups and the small-group experience that can make more-fluid small groups work. For example, a large men's service organization might offer an optional Bible study to members. In any given week, fewer than ten members of the ministry attend the Bible study, but they come with enough consistency for close friendships to form and meaningful conversations to be carried forward from week to week.

Small Groups Should Bear Fruit

The point of a small group is to raise up and strengthen apostles, to help the members grow in their maturity as Christians to the point at which they can identify their own callings and carry them out.

Some small groups should be dedicated to getting newly converted or reconverted Christians up and running with their freshly adopted Faith. Other groups should be dedicated to providing a place of support for seasoned Christians who have significant responsibilities (whether with a parish ministry or in work beyond the walls of the parish), and who need to bounce ideas off others who are doing similarly demanding work. Other small groups will serve a mix of people, typically centered more on a topical theme, whether that be parenting, serving the poor, studying a particular book of the Bible, staying sober, or any other common interest that draws a small group of people desiring to follow Jesus.

The objective of your small group might be something you know in advance, or it might be something you allow God to show you. Often it will be a combination of both. Perhaps you started with the objective of creating a group in which young fathers could pair with older men to learn more about how to live their lives as holy husbands and spiritual leaders in their homes. As the group got underway, you discovered, in listening to the men in your group, that there was a need to learn the basics of prayer; or a need to overcome addiction to pornography; or perhaps the need to go past the basics in the Faith for these already well-catechized and self-disciplined men and offer instead a place of rigorous study and encouragement to step out into serious Christian leadership.

Regardless of the composition of the group, an effective small group is one that causes people to grow stronger in their faith and to therefore act on that faith. A combination of one-on-one and small-group discipleship is the place where all your future leaders and volunteers come from.

Small Groups Take Many Forms

A small discipleship group can exist as a stand-alone concept in your parish. You can announce, "We are forming a small-group ministry. Groups are being hosted by five sets of leaders, meeting at different times and places. Sign up for the group that fits your schedule." Often in this case, the groups will all work through the same Bible study, so that the whole parish is studying together. Alternately, each small-group leader could create a unique proposal, so that parishioners could choose whether they want to attend the "Hors D'oeuvres with the Minor Prophets" group or the "Mountaintop Experiences, and by That We Mean There's a Gear List and a Conditioning Program" group.

Small groups can also naturally form outside of a designated small-group ministry. An ordinary Bible study that attracts a modest turnout can become an excellent small group, if the leader is open to allowing discipleship to happen. Certain lay associations, such as the Legion of Mary, are de facto small groups, already organized (intentionally) to provide a discipleship group for members. Any large ministry in the parish should be encouraged, if possible, to offer a small-group spin-off for members — for example, the St. Vincent de Paul Society members could be offered a chance to meet for a regular prayer and study group separate from the society's service activities, possibly even led by a nonmember who is gifted in leading small-group discipleship studies and wants to support the society in that way.

In evangelizing a parish, the pastor, if he is able to do so, can use a small-group format to mentor his ministry leaders, thus getting to know them better and forming them into stronger Christian leaders. Depending on the spiritual state of staff and ministry leaders, this may be an evangelizing group and not yet a true discipleship group. A group of this nature also helps parish ministry leaders communicate more effectively with one another and work as a team in carrying out the mission of the parish. In cases in which the pastor cannot or should not take on such a role, a second option is for parish ministry leaders to meet separately, under the leadership of a parochial vicar, a staff member, or even an outsider chosen for that role. And finally, in many cases, the best choice may be for each ministry leader to seek a mentor, a spiritual director, or an accountability partner outside of the parish leadership network.

Of all the many options, however, the easiest and most practical way to begin and to sustain parish-wide small-groups ministry is to encourage the informal creation of mini gatherings of disciples who like one another and enjoy spending time together.

> *"Those who sincerely accept the Good News,*
> *through the power of this acceptance and*
> *of shared faith therefore gather together in*
> *Jesus' name in order to seek together the*
> *kingdom, build it up and live it. They make up a*
> *community which is in its turn evangelizing."*
> — Pope Paul VI, *Evangelii Nuntiandi*, "On
> Evangelization in the Modern World," 1975

Where to Begin?

Membership in a mini community of disciples is a true need for every Christian. Close, deep, formative relationships with other disciples can occur outside the parish walls — in the family, among Christian friends who know each other from work or sports or school, or as part of a nonparish apostolate; still, the parish is by definition the place charged with forming local Catholics to answer their individual vocations. What are the implications of this?

From a practical perspective, this means that a top-down creation of a single small-groups program is unlikely to be manageable. In a parish of five hundred families, you are looking at creating and managing a hundred groups! That's insane!

And yet every member of those five hundred households

needs deep, meaningful spiritual friendships if that member is to grow in his or her relationship with Jesus Christ. How can this be possible?

The answer is that we have to start where we can. We who fill the pews can prayerfully invite two or three likely candidates from the parish (or beyond) to begin meeting for a Bible study at home, in the coffee shop, or perhaps in the break room at work before the rest of the office rolls in. Those who are already leading comparatively small parish faith-formation classes can work on subtly shifting the emphasis of each course toward facilitating discipleship or evangelization, as appropriate.

In most parishes at this stage in the game, unrolling a large-scale "small-groups" program is unlikely to be effective, for the simple fact that there will not be enough disciple-leaders available to take on a group. Pastors and ministry leaders can, in contrast, look for opportunities to encourage the creation of small discipleship groups on an ad hoc basis wherever small groups of disciples happen to gather as part of various parish activities.

What Are the Qualifications of a Small-Group Leader?

The number-one qualification required in a small-group leader is a deep, abiding, personal relationship with Jesus Christ in the Catholic Faith. No amount of training or certification can replace this one essential. This is the nonnegotiable.

From a practical standpoint, though, we can, very roughly, parse out three common types of small groups and the sorts of leadership skills each requires:

1. **Like-minded disciple friends gathering to-gether on an informal basis.** In this type of group, the members are all disciples, and they are people who like one another and get along with one another easily. No special leadership

skills are required to mediate conflicts because the group members have compatible personalities and interests. Members will use their various gifts to build one another up in the Faith, consulting outside expertise as they feel the need. This is not just the easiest kind of group to form; it is also the type that, ultimately, we want to become the norm in our parishes. Pastors can facilitate the formation of such groups by words of encouragement and a friendly, positive attitude toward such initiatives.

2. **Parish-based, formal groups populated by disciples.** These groups pull together individuals who may have diverse communication styles and starkly contrasting personalities, but who all share the common desire to grow in the Catholic Faith. Members are not struggling with basic questions about the reality of the Incarnation, the authority of the Church, or the moral teachings of Christianity — though there can still be significant differences in the types and intensity of struggles that members are working through. Groups of this nature require a study leader who is able to moderate discussions to ensure that one person doesn't dominate the conversation and to work through frustrations that arise from the quirks and callings that make each member unique. The moderator may or may not be the person who handles tasks such as sending out group emails or organizing food and drink for group events — it is well if tasks are shared among group members according to

their respective gifts.

3. **Even in a parish where informal, self-formed small discipleship groups have become the norm, there will always be a need for parish-sponsored small groups.** These groups provide a venue for new parishioners to get plugged into the parish community and create a gathering place for those who, for whatever reason, do not have a Christian friend group within or beyond the parish.

4. **Groups populated by some combination of disciples and nondisciples.** Many parish Bible studies and ministry-generated small groups will draw participants who are nowhere close to discipleship. Members may be longtime Catholics and active participants in parish life, but they are still operating at the trust or curiosity threshold. This can be true even of parish staff with pastoral responsibilities. If such a group is to help all members progress in their spiritual walk, the group leader needs a strong evangelizing skill set. This will include the ability to listen attentively for cues as to the spiritual needs of various members and the ability to host conversations that are fruitful for members at differing points along the thresholds of conversion.

Programs such as Alpha for Catholics or Jesus Is Lord* can be useful both for facilitating the spiritual growth of members and helping small-group leaders grow in their skills as evangelists; it is important to remember, though, that programs are not silver bullets and that prayerful, spirit-led soul-to-soul accompaniment remains the order of the day.

Answering the Leadership Challenge

Let's take a moment to contemplate our long-term vision for small discipleship groups, because in doing so, we'll see that we have a massive amount of work cut out for us. The long-term goals are these:

- Most parishioners are disciples of Jesus Christ — people who have dropped the nets and given their lives completely to loving God and serving him.
- The parish's primary role is in forming, equipping, and sustaining disciples who go out and proclaim the Good News to the world outside the parish.
- Some disciples work within the parish to receive and evangelize those who are not yet disciples.
- All members of the parish have some kind of one-on-one or small-group spiritual support, whether in the form of working with a spiritual director, mutually mentoring another disciple, or participating in a formal or informal discipleship group.

---

* Jesus Is Lord is a program developed at Saint William parish in Round Rock, Texas (https://st-william.org/programs) and used at the St. Mary's Catholic Center in College Station, Texas. Contact either location to learn more.

- Most members of the parish have several over-lapping discipleship-support systems, such as a close spiritual friendship with one particularly kindred soul and then several additional small discipleship communities formed in the parish, in the family, at work, at school, or as part of an evangelizing apostolate serving the wider community.

Whoa! Very few parishes today are anywhere close to this. We can no more get to this point by immediately unrolling a large-scale "small-groups" program than a baby could suddenly become a grown adult. Maturation and growth take time. Where to begin?

1. **Be honest about your own walk along the thresholds of conversion.** It is possible that you have read this far in the book because you are an active Catholic — even a parish leader —yet your own relationship with Jesus Christ is still in the early stages, like a seed that's dormant, waiting for the right soil and season in which to sprout. That's okay. I have repeatedly found that the normal, healthy response to the call to evangelize is to say, "Slow down! First I need to work on my own relationship with God!" Good. That is absolutely the best place to start. Allow God to set the pace.

2. **Form a one-on-one relationship or a micro group with a trusted spiritual friend.** If you have never been in a discipleship relationship, start small. Start by meeting with just one or two people who share your goal of growing clos-

er to Jesus and with whom it's easy for you to get along. This could be someone you've identified as a spiritual mentor, or it could be someone at a similar point spiritually who wants to take on the adventure of figuring out this whole discipleship thing together. Through this process, you will gain valuable experience that will equip you for the next step.

3. **Form just one small discipleship group.** This could be among friends you know from parish activities, among colleagues at work or classmates at school, among residents of your neighborhood, or as part of a formal parish ministry. This group will be a learning experience for you. It may be the beginning of lifelong spiritual friendships, or it might fizzle out in six weeks. Don't let that worry you. Trust God to use your early small-group experiences as a means of showing you important aspects of your calling as his disciple.

4. **Move to the next step as you are led.** We all have different charisms and callings. Is the Lord leading you to begin serving him in an evangelizing activity in your community? Do you find you have a natural gift for forming and leading small groups, or do you find that what you need is a stable group of close friends who meet privately to encourage one another? Does your role in the parish give you an opportunity to launch one or more small-group initiatives? Who are the leaders God has put in your path who have gifts needed to nurture a discipleship group?

There is no master plan in all this, other than your being responsive to the plan of the divine master. Evangelization and discipleship are long, slow, labor-intensive processes. If you are gifted in small-group leadership, a realistic expectation is that you will need to invest years — not weeks or months, but years — in the lives of just a handful of Christians, helping them mature in their faith, discover their calling, and begin their own work of evangelization. This should not discourage you. This is the model Jesus set for us, and he knew what he was doing.

For Reflection

- In your own words, what's the difference between credentials and certifications and equipping a disciple of Jesus Christ to evangelize?
- Have you ever been part of a regularly meeting group of Christians who truly challenged each other to grow in the Faith? What were the circumstances? What did you contribute to the group, and what did you receive?
- Are you currently part of such a group? If so, what is that group like?
- If not, how could you form one? Who would be an obvious group of people to get together with? Where could you meet, and when? What would be a simple focus for your group to get you started?

Saints for Evangelists
Venerable Edel Mary Quinn
As a young woman, Venerable Edel Mary Quinn (1907–1944) felt a calling to religious life, but because she suffered from tuberculosis, she could not join a religious order. Instead, she joined

the Legion of Mary and devoted herself to serving the poor in the slums of Dublin. The Legion of Mary is a lay association for Catholics who undertake a life of discipleship in the world, serving as catechists, visiting the sick, and doing other works of mercy as they spread the Gospel. In 1936, she became an envoy to East Africa, where she worked as a missionary, traveling extensively to share the Faith wherever she could find welcome and listening ears. During her seven years in Africa, Edel established hundreds of chapters of the Legion of Mary across the nations of eastern Africa, despite her constant battle with severe illness. She was known for her complete trust in God's providence and her absolute refusal to back down when obstacles arose in her missionary work.

24

Catechesis

In many parishes, religious education is the single largest ministry, putting more staff and volunteers to work than any other. What are some ways in which we can adapt our existing faith-formation programs to the needs of our parishioners for evangelization and discipleship? What are opportunities for members of the parish who aren't involved in religious education to support this key function of the parish?

Key Points

- It's not your imagination if it feels as if your parish's catechetical program faces an impossible task.
- An evangelizing outlook can transform any curriculum or class configuration.
- Logistical tweaks can increase opportunities for long-term relationship building and one-on-one evangelization and discipleship.
- In considering creative solutions to common

problems, one-soul-at-a-time thinking helps us
hold on to the big picture.

Catechesis is the everything topic of the Catholic Faith. As the
Catechism observes, "Quite early on, the name *catechesis* was giv-
en to the totality of the Church's efforts to make disciples, to help
men believe that Jesus is the Son of God so that believing they
might have life in his name, and to educate and instruct them in
this life, thus building up the body of Christ" (CCC 4). In other
words: it's not your imagination if it feels as if your parish's catechetical program is expected to be all things to all people. More
than that, the *Catechism* affirms that no matter what type of mission God has called you to, inside or far beyond the parish walls,
there's going to be a catechetical component to your interactions
with both non-Christians and fellow disciples.

Thus, when I speak here of "your" catechetical program, the
"you" applies whether you are the pastor, the program director,
a catechist, a parent, a student, or a concerned parishioner. Although, in some sections of this chapter, I'll be addressing challenges specific to traditional parish religious education, keep
reading even if you are not at all involved in that part of your
parish's work. The mindset and teaching tools of an evangelizing
catechist are relevant to every mission field.

Conditions on the Ground

The catechetical life is tough. I've been involved in Christian formation, in one form or another, for the past twenty years, and I've
worked with just about every age group and educational approach
out there. In addition to my own experience, I've spent these past
two decades listening to hundreds of parents, catechists, and
faith-formation directors from across North America and a few
from farther afield. A consistent picture emerges:

- Program staff are overworked and underpaid, and budgets are tight.
- It is hard to find volunteers to teach in parish faith-formation programs.
- It is a struggle to get buy-in from the individuals and families whom the parish religious-education program is supposed to serve.
- Students in a given class are all over the map spiritually, from passionate disciples to disaffected nonbelievers.

This is true whether your slice of the catechetical pie is baptism prep, traditional K–12 religious ed, RCIA, marriage prep, or adult faith formation. And if these challenges aren't enough, feelings run deep. The current program doesn't satisfy, but change terrifies. As much as I can (and do) spend countless hours writing about ideal approaches to catechesis, the reality is that transforming a parish's methods of faith formation has to be carried out prayerfully and prudently.

Meeting Your Students at the Well

To start, put yourself in the ancient Holy Land. It's the middle of the day, hot, lonely, and you've been walking since forever. You've just entered a Samaritan village familiar to you. As you approach the well to get a drink, you see Jesus talking to a woman. (We're in the Gospel of John, chapter 4.) You know her. She's from your parish, and let me tell you, her life is a wreck. The marriage tribunal has gone to a punch-card system, she has been married and divorced and remarried so many times. Her kids don't make it to class, and when they do, they have the most off-the-wall questions for the catechists. She never volunteers, never uses the envelope system, and she'll show up for the potluck, looking for a free meal, but somehow forget to bring a casserole, again. Why is Jesus even bothering with her? It's no use!

You retreat to a shady corner to wait this one out, and something unexpected happens: After all these decades of just-plain-nothing getting through her head, in a few short minutes she goes from hitting up Jesus for a handout to running his evangelization campaign in the village. Wait a minute — what?

The encounter with the woman at the well is a model for catechists. Let's see how:

- The Lord approaches the woman with love and hope. He knows her whole sordid life story, but he has not given up on her.
- He allows the conversation to get "sidetracked." He answers her questions as she poses them.
- His primary focus isn't on pointing out her failures; it's on proclaiming the kingdom.
- He chooses personally meaningful ways of proclaiming the kingdom to her (the living water leading to the question of worship and the arrival of the Messiah) that will resonate with her lived experience and tie her everyday needs to her deeper spiritual needs.
- As her heart is converted, he allows her still-in-formation, still-imperfect self to act on her newfound faith and start inviting others to hear the Good News.

We catechists, of course, are not the omniscient Son of God. We'll need much more time spent listening and building relationships, as well as a significant investment in prayer and fasting over our students as we evangelize and disciple them. Ultimately, as with the woman at the well, it is Christ drawing all things to himself that is the force of conversion, not our clever lessons.

But, switching points of view and now identifying ourselves with the woman at the well: The Lord lets us contribute our part to his missionary work. If we align our heart with the Lord's, our catechetical work can be evangelical work. Just as the woman at the well knew where to find the other villagers and what message would grab their attention, there are some catechetical skills we can deploy to draw those in our parishes closer to Jesus Christ.

> *"In catechesis, 'Christ, the Incarnate Word and Son of God, ... is taught — everything else is taught with reference to him — and it is Christ alone who teaches — anyone else teaches to the extent that he is Christ's spokesman, enabling Christ to teach with his lips.' "*
> — CCC 427

Making an Ordinary Lesson into an Evangelizing Lesson

Let's start with the most basic level of evangelizing catechesis. How can I evangelize more effectively the very next time I open my mouth to pass on the Faith, whether that's in the classroom or just answering a friend or a loved one's random question? The secret here is not in finding the perfect curriculum or the ideal teaching method. The secret is to internalize fully the Good News.

As you are speaking, no matter what your topic, put your answers in the wider context of that Good News. Let's use an example from a typical introduction or review session on the sacraments. As a disciple who is daily walking out your own relationship with the Lord, you can attest: The sacraments are all about your relationship with God and his saving relationship with you.

Relationships aren't passive. Though it is important to provide your students with concise definitions of the sacraments, you don't want to leave it there. When describing what happens in the sacraments, use active voice rather than passive voice.

Not enough: "In baptism, original sin is removed."

Explain further: "When you ask for baptism, you are asking God to come into your life and remove all sin from your soul. You are asking him to remove every barrier that separates you from him, so that you and the Lord can share the intimacy and loving bond that he created you to experience."

Not enough: "In the Sacrament of Reconciliation, mortal sins are removed and supernatural grace is bestowed upon the soul."

Explain further: "In the Sacrament of Confession, you are approaching Our Lord and asking him to forgive your sins. It is, in its essence, apologizing to Jesus. You are rebuilding your friendship with God, just as you'd have to do some 'rebuilding' if you'd had a fight with one of your friends, or with your mom or dad, or your spouse, or your child. The thing about the sacrament is that God is always, always, waiting for you to come to him, because he desperately wants to be in a relationship with you. You never ever have to worry that you've done something unforgivable. No matter how far you've gotten away from God, he always wants you back in his arms."

And so forth. How do you "come up" with these ideas? Meditate upon the sacraments. The theology is beautiful. When you are preparing your lesson, ask yourself: *How is this lived in my life? What do I experience when I approach God in this way?*

In some sense, every lesson you teach is simply your sharing your own testimony of God's work in your life. When you go to adoration, what do you feel? What do you seek? What do you receive? How are you changed? If you are teaching on the Sacrament of Matrimony, how has your experience of marital faithfulness and marital intimacy drawn you, and others, closer to Jesus Christ in his love of his Bride, the Church? Perhaps you are teaching a group of students about the various objects found in the parish church. How do the stories told or symbols contained in the artwork at your parish convey to you the love of God? How does the sacredness of the altar stir your heart when you contemplate Jesus Christ, the Lamb of God, broken for our sins? How does the sanctuary lamp (the candle near the tabernacle) beckon you to adore Jesus Christ, who has promised to remain with us always, even to the end of the age?

Let me emphasize here that it isn't a question of getting rid of boring definitions. Concise, technically accurate theological definitions are precious seeds for future contemplation. Your students need those hardworking rote definitions as fodder for their meditations. But in class, also give them a taste of the fruit of your relationship with the Lord. Give them a taste, through your evangelizing catechesis, of what awaits them if they choose to seek the Lord. Tell them stories of how your life has been changed by God and how they, as fellow disciples, can also grow closer to the Lord through their prayer and study, through the sacraments, and through their daily acts of service, regardless of their state in life.

Using Improved Logistics to Build Relationships

The next set of changes you can make — whether on a large scale or a micro scale — involve building deeper relationships with students and families in your parish faith-formation program. Jesus knew more than his message; he knew the person he was speaking to. Strong relationships are key to that one-soul-at-a-time process of evangelization and discipleship. To build those relationships, we need lots of time spent getting to know one another and living together as a community. There are things we can do in parish faith formation to allow that to happen more easily. Here, I will use examples drawn primarily from K–12 religious education, but think about how similar changes can apply in other age groups and other types of ministry, both in the parish and beyond.

- Can you arrange a drop-off and pick-up process that allows parents to meet their children's catechists face-to-face, with a cushion of free time for informal conversation?
- Can you organize the parish faith-formation schedule so that any given family can choose a single weekly slot for all members to gather, so that family schedules aren't stretched thin and dinner time isn't broken up several times a week?
- Can classes be organized so that students have the option of continuing with the same catechist for more than one year?
- Can a portion of your faith-formation program include intentional crossover with parish ministries that are conducive to conversation and friendship building?
- Can you create real-life or virtual "meeting places" where parishioners with common interests can meet each other, spend time together, and make plans?
- Can you incorporate faith-formation activities that encourage intergenerational get-togethers? (Holiday-related activities are ideal for this.)

These changes do not need to be elaborate or complicated. The simple change from a car-line drop-off system to parking and walking my child into class was the difference, for my family, between never meeting my children's instructors and easily recognizing the familiar face of a friendly catechist at parish events for years to come.

If you have the luxury of a spare classroom or a large lobby, putting out coffee or tea service will allow parents who would otherwise sit alone in their cars, checking their phones for an hour, to meet each other instead (have parents who participate clean up the beverage area fifteen minutes before dismissal). If your teen program meets on a different night from your elementary program, can you create an option for teens with siblings in the elementary program to serve as assistant catechists under the guidance of a pair of parent mentors (someone who has to come for drop-off and pick-up anyway) as an alternative formation program?

If nothing else, can you open the doors to your parish church so parents waiting on their kids can spend a few minutes building their relationships with the Lord in prayer before the Blessed Sacrament?

Creative Options for Catechetical Challenges

Before we begin this section, let's be very clear: Please don't fix what isn't broken. Whether you are in parish leadership, teaching, enrolling in classes, or a concerned parishioner, start with some assessment. What is already working well? What are the must-keep features of faith formation as it stands right now? Even if your current catechetical program is a sinking ship in heavy seas, there are likely valuable components worth rescuing.

Next, identify needs and wish-list items as precisely as possible. This could be purely practical ("I really need something on Tuesday nights" or "Our little kids are being kept up too late"); it could be spiritual ("The children don't attend Mass on Sundays" or "When we pray with our students, it doesn't feel as if we're connecting to God"); or it could be curricular ("We need more theology" or "There aren't classes suited to active students with a hands-on learning style"). Changing a catechetical program is a risky undertaking, so don't jump at a solution just because it's sparkly and different. Know what you're looking for under the hood, so to speak, so you can evaluate whether a given approach will meet your needs and so that members of the parish can work cooperatively in the give-and-take of developing a viable path forward.

With that prep work in mind, here are a few possibilities to consider as you brainstorm ways to meet the unique challenges your parish faces.

Catholic 101

This approach is ideal for parishes in which a significant number of students each year are just getting started in practicing the Faith. The standard course per diocesan catechetical progression guidelines or your chosen textbook series is offered by default, but beginning by third grade at the latest, students have the option of taking an age-appropriate entry-level intro to Catholic basics instead. Where volunteers are tight, to make this work you may need to move to combined-grade courses, an approach that is strongest when teachers aren't working straight from workbooks only, but are instead using any off-the-shelf materials as an outline and launching point for active learning.

VBS-style or workshop-style catechesis

Think about the typical VBS program: All students gather for an opening session, which includes music, group prayer, and an introduction to the key themes for the day. Then students break into smaller units to rotate through activities taught by specialists — Bible stories, games, crafts, and so forth. A simplified school-year adaptation might have students gather for a large-group assembly during drop-off and then break into smaller units built around either identified student needs (this group needs 101, this group needs intensive theology, this group needs high-energy learning activities) or identified catechetical strengths (he's a genius at getting kids to sing, she can hold a group spellbound with Bible stories). The outstandingly effective Catechesis of the Good Shepherd can fall under this umbrella as well.

Short courses and themed catechesis

Rather than offer a monolithic school-year-long curriculum, instructors can propose courses for shorter sessions (four-, six-, or eight-week cycles) that incorporate traditional catechesis into special-interest programs. One instructor might offer a study focused on saints; another might teach by using hands-on art projects; a third might lead students through a series of service activities. Offerings in any given cycle will be mixed-age, but the nature of the course will determine how tight or broad the age range is. Although this requires more logistical support from a skilled catechetical administrator up front, it has the advantage of harnessing specialized talents among parishioners and allowing catechists who can't commit to the entire school year to contribute their gifts on a shorter-term basis. Themed catechesis built on service, prayer, theology, church history, vocation prep, evangelization, or discipleship can, of course, be offered in year-long courses as well.

Family faith formation and supported home study

In the family approach, catechists teach parents the faith directly, and then parents use what they learn to teach their children in the home. FamilyFormation.net was one of the pioneers of this approach, which is now offered by a wide variety of Catholic curriculum providers, though I first learned about it from a missionary priest in Peru. In some parishes, catechists meet one-on-one with parents in the family home; in others, large-group sessions at the parish are organized so that families can get to know one another.

Summer programs

Summer can be used to offer far more than the basic VBS. Innovative parishes around the country report success with two types of expanded summer programs. One is offering the traditional school-year catechesis in a summer-intensive format over two weeks of full-day sessions, as an alternative to completing the same course of study during the school year. The second is an enhanced summer enrichment program; think VBS meets summer camp. The parish offers half-day camp sessions in the morning, with optional childcare in the afternoons for an additional fee, competitive in terms of price and activity offerings with local YMCA summer childcare and day-camp programs.

Student-led catechesis

The most radical departure from religious-ed-as-usual is especially suited to teens who are either struggling with their Faith (most) or are already disciples or seekers (quite a few). With this approach, a skilled mentor-catechist works with a small group of teens who take on personal responsibility for their faith. The mentor's role is to create a forum in which teens can honestly address their spiritual concerns and longings. Mentor adults facilitate teen-driven initiatives, whether for additional study, for learning ways to pray, or for carrying out evangelizing activities. Teens in the small group commit to supporting one another as a mini community growing together despite individual differences. Although most parishes are in no way ready to unroll this approach on a grand scale, it can be an excellent way to take pressure off traditional youth programs and meet individualized needs, if there is a parishioner capable of providing the type of guidance necessary for student-driven formation.

Though I have presented these ideas in terms of K–12 catechesis, think about how these ideas can be adapted to other needs or support intergenerational relationships. Adult faith formation often takes a workshop-style approach — can you build on that? Family faith formation doesn't have to limit itself to K–12 students and their nuclear family; it can be modified into a whole-parish ministry. How could the principles of student-led catechesis revolutionize RCIA or marriage prep? Could you simplify baptismal prep by opening up pertinent family-formation nights to young married couples and expectant parents, building relationships between new and more-experienced couples in the process, rather than rushing to catechize parents quickly when they're dealing with the stress of a newborn?

> *"Accordingly, the definitive aim of catechesis is to put people not only in touch but in communion, in intimacy, with Jesus Christ: only He can lead us to the love of the Father in the Spirit and make us share in the life of the Holy Trinity."*
> — Saint John Paul II, *Catechesi Tradendae*, 1979

Using a Q&A Specialist to Support Struggling Catholics

The heavy lifting in evangelism and discipleship happens one-on-one, but catechesis is almost always a group endeavor. Catechists struggle to balance the need to teach prescribed curriculum while knowing that the most important part of catechesis is answering the questions that students are asking right now — questions that may be completely unrelated to the topic on the syllabus. One way to deal with these challenges is to create a formal mechanism for fielding all the one-off questions that tend to either overload pastoral staff or else be left unanswered.

The Q&A person (or team) might be staff or a volunteer, clergy or layperson, but he or she possesses a few important gifts:

- strong listening skills
- a mature, tested relationship with Jesus Christ
- an accurate knowledge of the Catholic Faith and a gift for explaining that Faith in a charitable,

> inspiring way
> - an evangelist's ability to discern the question behind the question and identify next steps in helping someone grow closer to the Lord
> - a working knowledge of ministries that struggling Catholics may need to connect with, including contact information

Give this person a chair (and possibly a coffee cart). On religious-education nights or other times of the week when large numbers of parishioners gather, find an empty classroom, office, or corner of the hallway where those with random questions can meet with the Catholic Q&A specialist. The hours between Sunday morning Masses, especially if there is already a regular social event, such as coffee and doughnuts, are ideal for a tag team of Q&A specialists to work in relay.

Post signs, announce in the bulletin: If you're a parishioner trying to work through some difficulty, or just need an answer to a simple question, there are conveniently scheduled hours to meet with someone ready to help. If demand is high, you may need several volunteers available to take the easy cases so that the most difficult topics can be addressed by someone with strong pastoral skills. As with street evangelization (chapter 14), have on hand information about how to get practical help for meeting physical, spiritual, and psychological needs.

If the prospect of corralling volunteers is daunting, remember that you don't have to schedule the same volunteers every week — this is a good job for knowledgeable disciples who can't commit to full year-long ministry due to other vocational commitments, but are willing to come as they are able.

When Your Sacramental-Prep Students Are Atheists

Far too often, the children, teens, or adults sitting at Mass or presenting for a sacrament aren't there because of their own faith but in order to keep the peace with a family member. Some will say so openly; others politely avoid creating a stir, then make their exit when they get the chance. The problem is so widespread that I challenge you to find any gathering on the topic of catechesis in which this concern doesn't enter the discussion.

There is no magic formula for causing these students to convert into sincere disciples. What we do know is this:

- God, who pursues every human soul, has led this person to your parish.
- This person is made to be loved — by you and by God.
- In the distressing disguise of a jaded, lip-service-rendering heathen who dares to darken your parish doors, your mission has been ordained by God himself.

God is not a master who whips his slaves into outward shows of subservience. He is a lover who pursues his beloved with tenderness, passion, and perseverance. An evangelizing catechetical program, therefore, no matter what type of program or schedule it deploys, will have two essential traits:

- **Trust-building will be the foundation.** Remember, this is the first threshold on the path to discipleship. How can you, personally, help make your parish a safe, comfortable, welcoming place for those who may be struggling with intense doubts or thick-skinned indifference?
- **Honesty is respected.** Given your role in your parish community, what actions and conversations can help break down the pressure to be

> "good enough" or "give the right answer"? How can you encourage others at your parish so that they don't feel the need to hide doubts, concerns, and difficulties?

Fundamentally, a culture change is in order. The parish must shift from a culture of meeting objective specifications to living together as a community of persons, each building our relationship with God as we can. In making this change, we can't control every member of our parish, but we can control our own interactions with others.

Change is scary, and it takes time. Prudent, Spirit-guided discernment is the order of the day. And yet, in talking to countless Catholics from every corner of parish life, the overwhelming consensus is that spiritual needs are not being met. This is true of barely-Catholics, of practicing Catholics across the spectrum, and of those who are tasked with leading the parish or teaching the Faith. We know we want something more and different, even if we aren't yet sure what it is.

The catechetical program is often a parish's largest ministry, so it is an obvious place to begin. Giving ourselves the freedom to step prayerfully away from catechesis-as-usual can bring an immense sense of relief as catechists are empowered to finally do the thing they've been longing to do, thus answering their individual God-given vocations as disciples of Jesus Christ.

For Reflection

- Describe your parish's faith-formation programs as best you know them. What are the biggest problems you see? What are the greatest strengths?
- Where do you fit into the puzzle? Are you a parish leader? A catechist? A volunteer in another capacity? A con-

cerned parishioner? The student or a parent of a student?

- Catechesis is about growing in one's relationship with Jesus Christ. With that in mind, what would you say are the top three unmet needs bothering you right now?
- If you, personally, were to bring about one small change to make your parish's faith-formation program more evangelizing, what would that change be? Whom would you work with to make it happen?

Saints for Evangelists

Venerable Rafael Cordero

Venerable Rafael Cordero (1790–1868) was born into a poor family in Puerto Rico. His father was a former slave who had purchased his own freedom. Cordero was largely self-educated, and in 1810, he opened a school in his home, where he taught both academic subjects and the Catholic Faith. For fifty-eight years, his school served all children who wished to attend, regardless of race or ability to pay. The home where he operated his school is on the National Register of Historic Places of the United States.

25

Forming Disciples for Ministry

Year in and year out, we hear about the need for lay Catholics to take up their share of the work of the Church. But how do we transition from spoon-feeding passive fellow parishioners to becoming a team of disciples working together to carry out our God-given mission?

Key Points

- Raising mature Catholics means handing over real responsibility.
- Discipleship requires authentic Catholic community.
- Our goal is not to create generic Catholics but to identify each parishioner's gifts and calling.
- The parish is the home from which we go out into the world to evangelize and serve.

Just as the goal of a higher education is to prepare students to go out into the world and undertake serious, adult responsibilities, the goal in the school of faith is to raise mature disciples. Christ's plan when he said, "Go and make disciples" was not that a few elite specialists would be capable of running the parish for the hundreds of adults in the pews who were paralyzed by an incense-induced coma. God, who made us, knows that if we are able to hold down a job in the career world, we can hold down a job in the kingdom as well. But how do we get there? What is lacking that causes parish staff to know for a fact that most of the warm bodies coming to church each week aren't ready to step up to the mission field? Three things are missing, and we've talked about the first two:

1. Evangelization
2. Discipleship
3. Responsibility

Evangelization gives us our motivation: It is only after we have come to know Jesus Christ as Savior that we are ready to take our place in the kingdom of God. Discipleship teaches us how to function as Christian believers. We've discussed some important aspects of discipleship in the past few chapters, but we have a few more pieces of the puzzle to put in place. Once we've done that, we can talk about finding each disciple's mission — his or her responsibilities as members of the household of God.

As we have seen, discipleship requires forming deep personal relationships. Discipleship is, at its heart, the Christian life lived together. Chances are you've heard people use the word "community" when talking about parish life. What does that word really mean?

Living as a Community of Disciples

When the topic of loneliness and exclusion from parish life came up among a group of Catholic evangelists, I threw down the gauntlet: I don't think most of us have a real community at our parishes. Even those who seem so busy or involved don't necessarily have deep, lasting spiritual friendships.

I proposed the following quiz, to see if your parish really is your community. Don't count close family members in your answers.

- Do the people you sit near regularly at Mass know your first and last name? Do you know theirs?
- Do you share a meal of some type with another member of your parish at least once a week? (Staff luncheons don't count.)
- Is there someone you see at Mass who's pretty likely to greet you on your way out, give you a hug, and say it's good to see you — and you know that the person really means it?
- At least once a week, do you pray (outside of Mass) with one or more members of your parish for each other's personal intentions?
- Do you regularly get together with other members of your parish to study the Faith, talk about your personal growth as Christians, and encourage one another?
- Is there someone you can turn to for advice in your struggles with the Faith? Is that person someone you can count on to love you and be kind to you despite your faults, and also to help you work through your difficulties and grow closer to the Christian ideal? Can you contact that person freely, as needed, without feeling as if you are being a bother?
- Do you see other members of your parish out-

side of church activities? Daily? At least weekly?

- In your hobbies, sports, or pastimes, are you likely to encounter other members of your parish?
- When you want to have a good time, is there another member of your parish you get together with and have a lot of fun with?
- When you need to talk about what's going on in your life, do you have a trusted friend from your parish whom you call or get together with?
- If you had a crisis, would a member or members of your parish be there to help with rides, meals, housework, or other emergency needs?
- If you were in the hospital, would someone you know from your parish come to visit you?
- If you were sick, would other members of your parish notice you were missing from Mass? Would they know why you weren't present? Would they ask if there was anything you needed help with?
- Do you have confidence that when things get really bad, you can turn to the people of your parish for support?

Each of these is a mark of a fully functioning, healthy community. In human bodies and in communal bodies, health runs on a spectrum, of course, and in a fallen world, all bodies will struggle to some extent. As with any ideal, the goal isn't to despair because we'll never get there (this life will never be perfect), but to look for ways to move ourselves a little closer to what we know we were made for.

Still, some of these questions seem like impossible standards because we are so used to living without real community, anywhere, that we don't know what human community is supposed to be. Some of them seem impossible because we have set our standards for parish life so low that we may have abandoned even basic social skills, such as knowing each others' names.

Community Is Not Optional

Human beings need community. We need genuine, deep, lasting friendships. Every person longs to love and be loved, to know and be known. This need is so powerful that those who are deprived of loving family or friends will often do anything — anything — to create that feeling of belonging and being loved. Either the Christian community answers that need, or we are, at best, reduced to a Me-and-Jesus factory.

So how do you build community? By living together. It's our responsibility as Christians to each do what we can to find ways to live life together with our fellow parishioners.

Living Together Is Part of Our Mission

Creating community isn't one more item on the parish checklist. It is the fact of life of being the Body of Christ. Think about it: Your own body functions well only if all the parts live and work together.

This isn't some creepy Pod People thing, though. We aren't a cult that seeks to control every aspect of members' lives. On the contrary, our plan of evangelization is to go out into the world, hoping to invite into our lives all the different kinds of people whom God has made, even the ones who don't fit our idea of what a Catholic looks like.

What Is at the Center of Our Community?

If what draws us together as a parish community is a certain sense of style, or a standard of living, or even a common cultural background, we're doing it wrong. A community of disciples is centered on one thing and one thing only: Jesus Christ.

That doesn't mean we can't have groups in our parish that are focused on common needs, whether that be parenting, or sports, or ethnic heritage, or sobriety, or coping with same-sex attraction. In fact we want our parish to be the place we can find support and companionship as we tackle life's challenges, because that's part of how we make our community stronger. But all of these different mini missions have meaning and sticking power only if the reason we come together at the parish is that we are all here to worship Jesus Christ.

Discipleship Depends on Authoritative Teaching

As we tie together the techniques of evangelization and discipleship, we come back to the beginning. What does it mean to worship Jesus Christ? We return to the creeds. We return to the *Catechism*.

This is why I mention community last in a long series of chapters on evangelization and discipleship, even though evangelization and discipleship work well only when the parish community is strong. If I had put the community questionnaire at the start of the book, well-meaning Catholics would immediately set to organizing clubs and programs to get parishioners to spend more time together.

We want that, but we want community to be a result of evangelization and discipleship. First, we evangelize. The evangelist must have experienced personal conversion. Then the evangelist brings others into a relationship with Jesus Christ. Then, as a small group of disciples, we seek to build our lives around following Christ. Our small groups are brought together in the larger context of the parish community.

We do this because we long for the companionship of other disciples. We long for others who are delighted and awestruck by the same wondrous things we hear and see and feel when we pray the Mass or gaze in adoration or pore over the Scriptures.

In the very process of loving Jesus Christ together, Christian community is formed.

Discipleship Means Handing Over Real Responsibility

When you are filled with zeal for Christ, you want to know him and make him known. Your desire for this will be greater than any other concern. With the single-mindedness of a small child who needs to "go potty" during Mass, you'll let no obstacle get in your way. Neither fear nor respect for persons will keep you from your goal. You will co-opt for your mission any help you can find. You will, in your eagerness to see the Gospel proclaimed, find yourself wanting to put other disciples to work.

This is not parish life as usual. In the unevangelized parish, there are programs that need to be staffed. Ministry leaders seek to keep the programs going by finding volunteers to carry out the same tasks that were carried out by previous waves of volunteers. Often people are asked to volunteer with no regard for whether they would be any good at the job in question. Assignments are simplified so that any warm body can fill the role. Mediocrity ensues, and the ministry flounders.

In the evangelized parish, the situation is completely different. Disciples seek to identify and use the gifts God has given them to answer the calling he has given them. Each of us is called by God, one at a time, to fulfill his purpose for us. In the process of maturing in the Faith, we try to discover what our small-*v* vocations might be: How is God calling me, personally, to fulfill the mission to go and make disciples?

Am I called to a life of prayer and fasting? Am I called to a ministry of hospitality? Am I a natural for getting out on the streets and listening to strangers? Do I have a gift for bringing reverence and joy to the liturgy, or glorifying God in the fine arts? Do I have a unique talent or life experience that makes me able to create a landing place for a certain type of person seeking shelter and hope in the Church? Do I have practical skills that equip me for carrying out a particular work of mercy? Am I a skilled teacher or cook or handyman or administrator? What has God created me to do, and what has he not created me to do?

In a discipleship-driven parish, we must allow space for those gifts to be offered and have the courage to offer our own gifts. Prudence remains a virtue, but fear is not prudence. We encourage and foster new initiatives as parishioners propose them; after the Gospel pattern, we start small and low-risk and hand over greater responsibility as God leads and the disciple proves able.

While a parish with a strong spirit of discipleship will naturally have many opportunities for new believers to grow in their faith by working alongside mature Christians in parish ministry, the ultimate goal is not to staff parish programs. That will happen automatically, but it isn't the goal. The goal is to discern God's calling, knowing that in order to proclaim the kingdom, sometimes that calling will be far beyond the parish walls.

> **"Within the Communion of the Church, the
> Holy Spirit 'distributes special graces among the
> faithful of every rank' for the building up of the
> Church. Now, 'to each is given the manifestation
> of the Spirit for the common good.' "**
>
> — CCC 951

Discipleship Means Letting Go

When my son was seventeen, I took him and his youngest sisters to France for a month. A year later, he asked for a bold gift for his eighteenth birthday: Would his father and I help fund a return trip for him — solo this time?

This is what young adults do. Some of them go off and get their own apartments. Some of them take summer jobs on the other side of the country. Some of them hit the road and travel around.

I knew he could do it, because I had taught him. He had done international flights and trains and public transit. He'd done hotels and apartments and restaurants and grocery stores and hut-to-hut hiking. He was familiar with the French obsession for regulation headshots slapped on anything and everything, and how to hunt down a photo booth when you need one. He had even demonstrated his ability to read a French neighborhood and know whether it was one that nonlocals should be wandering in.

What he hadn't done is do the thing all by himself, with his parents tucked away on another continent. Of course not — he had just turned eighteen.

I held my breath and reminded myself that the whole point of parenting is to raise young adults, and he had reached the age when he was ready to start doing adult things.

So we made a budget, and off he went.

Problems came up, as happens when you travel. Some he solved with admirable skill, and others he muddled through as best he could. He came home with a list of things he'd do differently next time and an impressive list of ways he had made the most of his trip.

He had reached maturity as a disciple in the art of travel.

Like nervous parents watching their children fly the nest, it can be hard to let Christian disciples head out on their own. Just as parents can coddle a grown child into learned helplessness, so can Christian leaders coddle their parishioners, and we parishioners can let ourselves be coddled. We who read about the mishaps of the apostles as told in the Gospels can appreciate that Christ might have been cringing omnisciently even as he breathed on the Twelve and gave them their mission.

And yet that is God's plan for the world: that we fallible humans would bungle our way through proclaiming the kingdom and bringing others to Christ.

For Reflection

- In your own words, what is the difference between a community built around a shared love of Jesus Christ and other types of community experiences?
- When you think of the "priesthood of all believers," what does that look like to you? Keeping in mind everything we've learned about evangelization, what are some concrete examples of ordinary lay Catholics carrying out their Christian vocation?
- Do you tend to be a risk-taker or a risk-avoider? How does that impact your willingness to stand up for Christ?
- Who do you know who loves Jesus wholeheartedly but feels unqualified to evangelize? How can you help that person to discover and carry out his or her mission in proclaiming the Gospel to the world?

_____

Saints for Evangelists

Blessed Hermann of Reichenau (September 25)

Blessed Hermann of Reichenau (1013–1054) was son of the Count of Althausen, a town in southern Germany. His parents sent him at the age of seven to be educated at the nearby Benedictine monastery, which, at the time, was a major center of European intellectual life. He chose to join the order at the age of twenty and later became abbot of the monastery.

The extensive scope of Hermann's work is an example of how any field of study or profession can be part of a disciple's mission territory. He was literate in multiple languages and was instrumental in introducing science and technology from Arabic Spain to Central Europe. He was known for his liturgical compositions and his extensive writings in music, science, theology, and history. One of the marks of his scholarship is the combination of both theory and practical application in the subjects he studied, leading to an astonishing diversity of genres of his writing. His best-known work today is the Salve Regina, though the final line ("O clement …") was reportedly added by Saint Bernard of Clairvaux upon hearing the hymn for the first time.

Conclusion
Unleashing the Church Militant

Jesus came to call not the righteous, but sinners. My expertise is in being one of those sinners who keeps getting called.

I am an ordinary Catholic. I belong to an ordinary parish, led by priests who are very good at a few things and who trust in the grace of God for the rest. In the pews are other ordinary Catholics like me, trying to pray more and sin less, love more and complain less, and, on any given week, counting it a victory if we manage just to get ourselves where we need to be, more or less on time.

If you were looking for a book about how to build an international speaking career, or how to run a multimillion-dollar evangelizing ministry, there are other authors for that. This book is about how to be an ordinary Catholic who evangelizes.

Like you, I have things I'm good at and things I'm not very good at. Evangelization is not a one-man show.

And that brings us to the beauty of spiritual gifts: you have read something in this book that made a light bulb go off. You read about some part of evangelization or discipleship that immediately got your mind turning. "I could do that!" you said. "That would be fun! Wow! What a great idea!"

Go do that thing.

> *"May no adversity paralyze you. Be afraid*
> *neither of the world, nor of the future, nor of*
> *your weakness. The Lord has allowed you to live*
> *in this moment of history so that, by your faith,*
> *his name will continue to resound throughout*
> *the world."*
> — Pope Benedict XVI, World Youth Day, August 2011

God will give you the size of ministry he wants you to have. He will give you the amount of success he wants you to have. He will give you the amount of sleep, the amount of support, and the amount of coffee you need in order for you to carry out his divine will.

God is calling you. He's either calling you to be a famous evangelist, or he is calling you to be a not-famous evangelist. You don't need to know which. Try the thing you read about that caught your imagination. Our Lord has gone before you, and he has promised that you do not need to be afraid.

Acknowledgments

The list of people I'd like to thank runs into the thousands, starting with Mom and Dad, and if you understood, at all, how blessed with friends and family and colleagues and acquaintances and strangers that I have been in this life, you would notice that we aren't in eternity quite yet, so the unabridged thanking will have to wait.

Meanwhile, limiting ourselves strictly to bookishness: Christian LeBlanc gets the credit for talking me into reading *Forming Intentional Disciples* way back in 2012, and Sarah Reinhard's involvement in making this book happen goes back much further than either of us are likely to remember, certainly not before coffee.

Sherry Weddell and Katherine Coolidge from the Catherine of Siena Institute have been educating me and thousands of others through their work at the Forming Intentional Disciples discussion forum, where they regularly share links, stories, and discussion prompts about all aspects of evangelization and discipleship.

My blog readers and Facebook friends have provided answers to many questions I posed in writing this book. Thank you to hundreds of readers who shared favorite saints, personal stories of evangelization and discipleship, experiences with parish access for persons with disabilities, and countless other ideas that find form in this book, directly or behind the scenes. Your help has been invaluable.

In addition to the helpfully organized documents at Papal-Encyclicals.net and my own (unhelpfully disorganized) library, quotes from Church documents are courtesy of Keith Strohm, Jaymie Stuart Wolfe, Melanie Bettinelli, Mary Hathaway, Judy Campbell, Marcel LeJeune, and, opening the floodgates of inspiration, Carole Brown.

This book's chief editor, Rebecca Willen, gets the gold star for patiently pointing me back in the right direction as I veered off the road again and again in the original manuscript.

Beyond those few names? Countless friends who have guided and assisted and prayed me this far, and I am grateful for every one of you. There isn't enough paper to name you all.

It will have to suffice, for now, to leave off by thanking my top four mentors in the Faith, who never give up on attempting to rectify my erroneous ways and who are in my life thanks to #5, who endures, sacrifices, and grows daily in holiness through all the opportunities I so effortlessly provide for him in his quest to practice heroic virtue. Thank you.

About the Author

JENNIFER FITZ loves Jesus Christ, writing, teaching, and playing outside. She is the author of *Classroom Management for Catechists* and the *Lord, You Know I Love You* discernment retreat, and a contributor to numerous other Catholic books, periodicals, and websites. She has taught the Faith in just about every format possible over the past twenty years, to every age group, from young children to retirees, including traditional parish faith-formation programs (K–12 and adult), homeschool cooperatives, a private Christian school, family-to-family discipleship groups, and as a chastity-education presenter for Family Honor. She has a BA in International Studies and an MBA from the University of South Carolina, and a *Certifact d'Etudes Politiques* from Sciences-Po Paris. Find her online at the *National Catholic Register* and at her personal blog, jenniferfitz.com.